"Mark Cox's new book *Lear
and leading are two sides o
heart and purpose. You wi.
service-oriented sales."
—**Kevin Cashman**, Vice Chairman, CEO & Enterprise Leadership,
Korn Ferry, best-selling author of *Leadership from the Inside Out*

"Mark Cox has decades of experience selling, training salespeople,
and coaching sales managers. He has distilled that wisdom into a
terrific book that covers core topics from identifying target customers and articulating a value proposition to crafting a repeatable
sales process and relevant management practices. *Learn to Love
Selling* is, in the best sense, a playbook—a realistic and flexible set
of actionable guidelines, not another rigid 'methodology.' It also
provides many downloadable tools to embed those guidelines in
your organization. Whether you are an early-stage entrepreneur or
a senior sales manager or rep at a big corporation, read and learn
from Mark's book."
—**Frank Cespedes**, Harvard Business School, best-selling author
of *Sales Management That Works: How to Sell in a World That Never
Stops Changing*

"This is a book on modern selling. Many sales books out there
are based on a pre-internet, pre-COVID world; they won't get you
far. Mark Cox has created a book to give you a sales strategy and
tactics to be a sales success in the fast-paced, modern world."
—**Tim Hughes,** CEO and Co-Founder of DLA ignite, best-selling author of *Social Selling: Techniques to Influence Buyers
and Changemakers*

"In *Learn to Love Selling*, Mark Cox provides the steps to increase your sales, build a formidable sales team, and achieve remarkable results. Sales training is one of the most beneficial things anyone can receive to develop empathy, the ability to formulate benefits, articulate a clear value proposition, and communicate effectively with potential customers. Mark Cox has mastered the art of sales training through lessons from top thought leaders and sales professionals. He shares critical takeaways to ensure you avoid common pitfalls and elevate your sales game. Get ready to boost your sales and achieve success beyond your wildest dreams."
—**Dr. Diane Hamilton**, Business Behavioral Expert, best-selling author of *Curiosity Unleashed*

"Mark Cox created a comprehensive guide that promises to transform how you approach B2B sales. Authored with a deep understanding of the modern sales landscape, this groundbreaking book is structured to provide both novice and seasoned sales professionals with actionable insights and strategies to excel in their profession.

This book is not only impactful for the mind to design and deploy new strategies, but it also helps rekindle the reader's love for the selling profession. Filled with compelling personal stories and immediately useful graphics, this book offers an easy-to-apply blueprint to convert a product into predictable revenues.

This is a refreshingly useful, easy-to-read handbook filled with hundreds of practical insights, time-tested concepts, and action steps. It is a must-read for anyone whose income depends on generating revenues."
—**Gerhard Gschwandtner,** Founder and CEO, *Selling Power* magazine

"Whether you are new to sales or an experienced sales leader, *Learn to Love Selling* by Mark Cox will fill in the gaps and speed you toward greater sales results in B2B sales, ensuring you love selling more than ever."
—**Anthony Iannarino,** Managing Member of Iannarino Fullen Group and best-selling author of *The Negativity Fast: Proven Techniques to Increase Positivity, Reduce Fear, and Boost Success*

"*Learn to Love Selling* by Mark Cox is a must-have guide for anyone in the B2B sales arena. It's filled with practical strategies and insightful tactics that are easy to implement. Mark's expertise shines through every page, providing a clear road map to sales success. This book will change the way you approach selling, making it a more enjoyable and rewarding experience."
—**Justin Michael**, Co-Founder and CRO of Hard Skill Exchange, best-selling author of *Attraction Selling: Unleashing the Law of Attraction to Multiply Sales Results with Music, Sleep, and the Justin Michael Method 3.0*

"A thread runs throughout Mark's new book, *Learn to Love Selling*, which is at the very core of all successful sales approaches. Mark correctly states, 'In professional sales, everything must be focused on how you can help your prospect achieve a desirable business outcome. It's always about them, not you.' Once you embrace this sales truth, you can put Mark's sales playbook to work.

Mark covers the essential plays with relatable stories and practical examples. The best part is that you will truly love to sell as you deploy the plays, which naturally leads to a successful career in sales."
—**Lisa D. Magnuson**, LinkedIn Learning Instructor and Complex Deal Sales Consultant/Strategist, best-selling author of *The TOP Sales Leader Playbook: How to Win 5X Deals Repeatedly*

"In *Learn to Love Selling*, Mark Cox has accomplished the near-impossible task of writing a concise, easy-to-read sales book that is also a comprehensive single-volume guide for sellers and sales managers to learn the skills, tactics, and strategies they need to master to take their careers to the next level."

—**Andy Paul**, Founder of Zero Time Selling Inc., best-selling author of *Sell Without Selling Out: A Guide to Success on Your Own Terms*

"B2B selling starts with the customer and not with the product. However, way too often, sellers still neglect this ultimate truth. With *Learn to Love Selling*, Mark Cox offers hands-on, practical advice and tools to overcome the product focus and become more customer-centric."

—**Christoph Senn**, Adjunct Professor of Marketing, INSEAD, Co-Director of the Marketing & Sales Excellence Initiative

"*Learn to Love Selling* by Mark Cox is a transformative read for anyone in the sales profession. It perfectly balances practical advice and strategic insights, making it an invaluable resource for newcomers and seasoned sales experts. The actionable tips and real-world examples make it an engaging and enlightening guide that can significantly boost your sales career."

—**Hermann Simon**, Founder and Honorary Chairman of Simon-Kucher, best-selling author of *Confessions of the Pricing Man: How Price Affects Everything*

"Mark Cox has jam-packed pure sales and management gold nuggets into *Learn to Love Selling*. Sales leaders and sales pros alike will benefit from page after page of actionable strategies and tactics. All are presented in an easy-to-read style with examples and personal stories that bring the material to life.

Plus, the extra bonus material he offers is worth far more than the small investment in the book. Add this to your 'A-list' of sales books."
—**Art Sobczak**, Founder of Business By Phone Inc., best-selling author of *Smart Calling: Eliminate the Fear, Failure, and Rejection from Cold Calling*

"This book is everything you would want in a sales playbook. It's practical, pragmatic, and precise.

Learn to Love Selling does what it says on the tin, clearly written by someone who knows and loves the profession. Mark authentically draws not only on his personal experience but from subject matter experts he respects—it's a compelling and great read."
—**Dr. Philip Squire**, CEO of Consalia, best-selling author of *Selling Transformed: Develop the Sales Values Which Deliver Competitive Advantage*

"This is a go-to, MUST READ, for people looking to invest in their sales career development. Mark's expansive knowledge and skill sets will guide you into the sales funnel on facilitating, managing, and leading innovative sales teams and processes in today's modern advanced sales environment. We are no longer living in the 1980s consultative sales manipulative schemes. This book brings you to today and prepares you for the future."
—**Dr. Grant Van Ulbrich**, Founder of Scared So What Ltd., best-selling author of *Transforming Sales Management: Lead Sales Teams through Change*

LEARN TO LOVE
SELLING

THE UNIVERSAL B2B SALES PLAYBOOK

MARK COX

IN THE FUNNEL™
PUBLISHING

IN THE FUNNEL™
PUBLISHING

Learn to Love Selling

Paperback ISBN: 978-1-0688565-1-8
e-Book ISBN: 978-1-0688565-0-1

Cover design by Julia Kuris • designerbility.com.au
Interior layout by Kristy Twellmann Hill • umbrellasquared.com

Printed and bound in Canada.

inthefunnel.com

ACKNOWLEDGMENTS
AND GRATITUDE

I LOVE learning.

This love of learning came from my mum and dad.

My parents (David and Nancy) were British baby-boomer immigrants to Canada who wanted better lives for their children than they had. They invested heavily in their children's educations, and I was privileged to learn in some of the best schools in the world.

I loved learning then and still do. They are the reason why.

In life, there are three simple but very important questions we all need to address to be happy:

1. Who do you love?
2. What do you do?
3. Where do you live?

I have been most lucky with number one.

Thank you to the love of my life, Donna.

Thank you for your love, friendship, support, and caring. Your unwavering confidence in my abilities and ambitions is oxygen for me, especially when my confidence wavers (which it does).

You are still the one I want to "show off" for most, whether writing a book, running a business, playing drums in a bar band, or trying to make you laugh with my surprisingly immature sense of humor.

One of my favorite sounds in the world is your laugh, which I hear often.

I have also been so very lucky to land on number two, running IN THE FUNNEL© for the last ten years.

After many years leading sales organizations in outsourcing or technology companies, I took the risk of starting a sales training company. Then I realized how much I truly enjoyed coaching people and seeing others develop. It is a true labor of love and allows me to work on my terms with my unique ability.

Running IN THE FUNNEL has also allowed me to work with some of the top entrepreneurs, CEOs, sales leaders, and salespeople in the world.

Thank you to our amazing customers for the privilege of working with you, learning from you, and being inspired by you. I have referenced only a very small portion of you in the book, but all of you inspire me.

Ten years ago, I would never have made the transition from corporate executive to entrepreneur without the incredible support of my mentor, Ian Sutcliffe.

It is rare to meet successful people in the corporate world who care more about your personal and professional development than their own, but Ian Sutcliffe is truly one of those people. Ian, you have been an amazing mentor and friend. Thank you.

I'd also like to thank all of the teammates who have worked as part of IN THE FUNNEL over the years. Thank you for investing your career with us and for all of the contributions you have made.

I'd like to thank Sandra DeSouza for your unwavering commitment to helping us execute our mission, which is to elevate the performance and professionalism of B2B sales and, by doing so, improve the lives of professional salespeople.

Sandra, you are an amazing friend to Donna and me. Thank you.

Writing this first book has been quite a journey, and there are predictable ups and downs as we get to the endgame. We've worked through the bankruptcy of our first publisher and COVID-19.

Special thanks to Dave Hanley, a client, friend, and teammate who helped reengage this process when we hit some paralyzing procrastination. Dave's energy, enthusiasm, and calm wisdom were critical to help us keep the pedal to the metal in the final stages of this process.

Kevin Winters has always done an amazing job of turning our ideas into beautiful models, tools, and workbooks. Thank you, Kevin!

I'd also like to thank and acknowledge some of the top thought leaders in the professional sales and business industry who have knowingly or unknowingly taught and inspired me along my professional sales journey, including but not limited to: Frank Cespedes, Andy Paul, Trish Bertuzzi, Robert Miller, Stephen Heiman, Jeb Blount, Matt Dixon,

Brent Adamson, Daniel Pink, David Ulrich, Roger Martin, Justin Michael, Hermann Simon, Stephen M. R. Covey, Dan Sullivan, Babs Smith, Jason Jordan, Michelle Vazzana, Anthony Iannarino, Carol Dweck, Geoff Smart, and Randy Street.

Finally, thank you. The growth-oriented entrepreneur, sales leader, or salesperson who invested in yourself by buying and reading all (please and thank you) of this book.

I sincerely hope you get enormous value from the strategies, processes, and tools that I have spent a lifetime developing and curating. If you need help refining them for you and your industry, reach out to me at markcox@inthefunnel.com and I will be delighted to help.

Let's learn to love selling!

This book is dedicated to the love of my life, Donna. Thank you for being my soulmate, best friend, coach, supporter, cheerleader, and life partner. If I had Marty McFly's time machine, I would do it again with you.

"Learning never exhausts the mind."
—Leonardo da Vinci

A NEW BEGINNING

As I drove to my first day of work in the heart of downtown Toronto, a rush of excitement mixed with nerves filled the air inside my brand-new company car—a sleek green Ford Taurus station wagon. The Toronto-Dominion Bank tower loomed before me as I walked into the lobby, feeling like a character out of a Wall Street movie with slicked-back hair and suspenders complementing my navy-blue BOSS suit and crisp white shirt.

Finally, after months of training, I had landed a role as a professional salesperson at Eastman Kodak. As I stepped into the office on the thirty-ninth floor, I settled into my desk, took a deep breath, and pondered the daunting question, "What am I supposed to do now?"

The initial months were a blur of fear and uncertainty. Despite being crowned the "Demo King of North America" during training (complete with trophies to prove it), I constantly worried about being exposed for not knowing what I was doing.

I knew how to demo and was pretty good when an existing client wanted to upgrade their photocopiers. However, the training completely avoided three critical components to selling:

1. What was the true value proposition of our capabilities to the client?
2. What was the Ideal Customer Profile?
3. Outside of demoing a photocopier, what were the exact steps to gain consensus from a buying group to purchase our technology?

There are countless books on professional sales. They address a myriad of topics from opening and closing deals to managing buyer groups and leveraging social media. I've read hundreds of these. Many are amazing, and I've interviewed their authors on my podcast *The Selling Well*.

Yet, none provided a comprehensive playbook on converting any product or service into revenue. Nobody has created the simple sales playbook that every salesperson can leverage regardless of their product, service, or industry.

That's why I wrote this book.

Thank you for choosing to read it.

In the following chapters, I'll share four fundamental steps every salesperson must take to convert any product or service into revenue:

1. Understand your value proposition to your target market.
2. Prioritize the pursuit of your target market.
3. Generate demand within your target market.
4. Win deals with a disciplined sales process and sales strategy.

It sounds straightforward because it is. Mark Twain once said, "I didn't have time to write a short letter, so I wrote a long one instead." I've taken the time to distill a concise, effective sales methodology applicable to every B2B salesforce across all industries.

However, simplicity doesn't equate to easiness.

Mastering professional sales is akin to running a marathon—simple in concept, extremely challenging in execution. Success requires a mindset of continuous learning and progress measurement, not perfection-chasing.

Yet, with the right guidance, selling can become an enjoyable journey focused on improvement.

After twenty-five years in sales, I continue to hone my craft with a newfound passion for learning and growth.

Welcome to the journey.

INTRODUCTION

Sales is the most essential function in business.

Chances are, if you keep reading, you are either a CEO, a sales leader, or in professional sales.

Ask yourself: "If we had sold twice as much last year, how would I feel right now?" The answer: *Spectacular*.

This is not arrogance or indulgence. It is simply a fact. If you are the CEO of a business, you know this. If you are an entrepreneur, you live this. If you are a sales manager or a salesperson fighting for deals on the front lines, your job security and career depend on this.

Dan Sullivan—founder of Strategic Coach and one of the world's leading authorities on entrepreneurship—likes to say, "If you can write a check to solve a problem, you don't have the problem." This is true from the earliest-stage start-ups to small- and mid-sized businesses and up to the world's largest publicly traded companies.

The problem is that too often, organizations don't grow. Entrepreneurs can't build successful sales teams, and sales leaders don't understand what they must do to accelerate revenue growth within their teams.

It goes without saying that the power of your sales will ultimately determine the success or failure of your business. Selling well really matters.

Everyone Sells

When asked by our fifth-grade teachers what we wanted to be when we grew up, few of us identified "salesperson" as our desired future. But many of us ended up here.

Approximately one in nine people in the United States is employed in a professional sales job.[1] This staggering number excludes all of us who spend much of our time *selling* but don't have "sales" in our job titles, like president, vice president, director, lawyer, accountant, consultant, or any other type of entrepreneur who regularly speaks with customers and prospects to drive revenue.

More are entering professional sales. According to Harvard's Frank Cespedes, in his terrific book *Sales Management That Works: How to Sell in a World That Never Stops Changing*, "Fifty percent of US college graduates, regardless of their majors, will work in sales at some point in their careers."[2]

With so many of us landing in sales in a roundabout way, the side effect is that we often take for granted that excelling in this profession means we must focus on lifelong learning and ongoing improvement. In this highly competitive field, the stakes are high when we're compensated according to our wins.

There is a way to sell effectively and efficiently. It's called the sales playbook.

Understanding the sales playbook is critical for the success and survival of sales leaders, professional salespeople, and entrepreneurs.

So, let's talk about why more salespeople aren't trained in this methodology, and why the discipline of professional sales suffers as a result.

Why the Sales Profession Is Not Performing Well

Changing buyer behaviors, evolving digital buying technologies, and the epidemic of ineffective sales behaviors have culminated in a breaking point in professional sales. We need a common-sense revolution to fix it *now*. We can no longer tell ourselves the same old stories, default to automation to sell on our behalf, and cite the same tired excuses to justify underperforming. An effective sales playbook is the only solution.

You may think your product, service, or pricing model matters...and it does. But the truth is, *how* you sell is at least as important as *what* you sell. In fact, according to a *Harvard Business Review* article, "Thirty-nine percent of B2B buyers select a vendor according to the salesperson's skills rather than price, quality, or service features."[3]

Let that sink in. Almost 40 percent of the time, the salesperson's skill overshadows the price, quality, and service features of what you sell.

Selling well really matters.

And yet, about 50 percent of salespeople miss their goals,[4] and more than half are looking for a new job right now.[5] The average sales leader lasts less than two years in their role.[6] Of course, these three phenomena are related.

And buyers don't want to interact with salespeople. According to the Gartner Group, buyers are spending less and less time with sales reps: "Only 17 percent of the total purchase journey is spent in such interactions." In fact, 44 percent of millennial buyers prefer no inter-action with a sales rep.[7] Why are so many people failing at sales? Because sales as a profession has no standard operating procedures to guide best practices across the discipline.

Professional sales is not consistently taught in colleges or universities with a formal curriculum. If you search any MBA program, you will see the curriculum littered with courses covering finance, supply chain, marketing, product development, operations, and human resources. Each of these disciplines has standard operating procedures, which will be taught in these classes, allowing the graduates to get a running start in their careers. Sales? Not so much.

Being professional in sales is also critically important for all entre-preneurs. Regardless of how good your product or service is, your business will die if you can't sell it.

Most entrepreneurs don't come from a professional sales background. They typically have a deep background in the function of their business. For example, tech entrepreneurs often start as application develop-ers, or manufacturing entrepreneurs as engineers. Entrepreneurs in professional service firms have backgrounds in the services they sell (law, accounting, consulting).

Even the best entrepreneurial companies struggle with sales at some point. Babs Smith is co-founder of Strategic Coach along with her part-ner Dan Sullivan. Strategic Coach is the top entrepreneurial coaching program for successful, growth-oriented entrepreneurs worldwide. Full disclosure: I am a huge fan of this company and have been a mem-ber for five years. Strategic Coach also has one of the finest company cultures that I have ever seen. In fact, I was so impressed with it that I encouraged my wonderful niece to apply to work there (and *yay* they were smart enough to hire her!).

But when they initially engaged IN THE FUNNEL© a few years ago, the sales organization needed some work. In Babs's words, "All of a sudden, it became apparent to me that our sales process was all over the map... we had grown but were hitting a plateau."

The reason? There was no consistent playbook for the sales team to be successful. They relied on a small number of salespeople knocking it out of the park—carrying the sales performance for the rest of the team. They were also defaulting to a high-end order-taking approach to sales because the brand was incredibly strong, and marketing provided huge numbers of well-qualified leads.

We (IN THE FUNNEL) assessed their go-to-market approach, identified the five areas that could have the most impact on improving sales performance, and helped Babs and her sales leadership teams build a playbook for achieving growth.

The result? Strategic Coach continues to have record-breaking growth year over year.

Referring to the ITF Sales Playbook, Babs said, "What we ended up getting was a whole sales management structure that we have never had before. We have a 10X goal and I feel way more confident now about getting there than I did at this time last year," before working with IN THE FUNNEL.

This playbook consistently drives top-tier sales growth for businesses in many industries whose success hinges on having an effective B2B sales team. We have implemented this simple but powerful sales system in dozens of companies and taught it to thousands of salespeople. The good news is that it is simple, and it works.

The IN THE FUNNEL Difference

Why am I qualified to educate both entrepreneurs and salespeople? I've spent over twenty-five years in professional sales. I have personally sold, structured, and negotiated billions of dollars in business, including a single deal worth a billion dollars. I have spent my corporate career leading sales organizations. I've run IN THE FUNNEL Sales Coaching for the last ten years, coaching hundreds of sales leaders and training thousands of salespeople to improve sales performance dramatically and, in doing so, improve the lives of those in professional sales.

I started IN THE FUNNEL Sales Coaching to elevate the sales profession and simply *help companies sell better*. My primary objective in writing this book is to give you a standard set of operating guidelines to help you sell better, whether you are an entrepreneur, sales leader, or salesperson. In short, this book teaches you the optimal, universal B2B sales playbook.

I've always seen a very close connection between entrepreneurs and salespeople. The best salespeople have always treated their territories like their own business and taken an entrepreneurial approach to achieving their sales objectives. Conversely, the best entrepreneurs understand that they are the company's chief sales officers.

If you are a sales leader, salesperson, or even an entrepreneur, this book will help you ace your sales goals in three ways:

- guide you to build the sales playbook to accelerate revenue growth in your business
- coach you to build the right sales team to execute that sales playbook
- educate you on how to lead the team to achieve amazing results

Part 1 will start with the IN THE FUNNEL Sales Playbook based on experience, research, best practices, and (perhaps most importantly) common sense. This playbook will clarify what you need to do to be the company that sells better than your competitors. Each chapter will provide practical exercises to apply the concepts, and online learning tools you can download to configure our playbook for your business.

You'll start by creating your business's value proposition. Next, you will prioritize the target market you will pursue after identifying your Ideal Customer Profile (ICP). You will then learn how to create demand for your services from that target market intentionally. Finally, you will learn the sales process and sales strategy that will help your prospects move along their buyer's journey and select you as their solution.

In Part 2, we will review best practices for building the right sales team to execute your sales playbook. You will create job descriptions and then recruit, interview, hire, and properly onboard new salespeople into your business. We will also discuss an appropriate ramp-up period to give them enough time and education to be successful.

In Part 3, we will review how the right sales-management cadence will allow you to execute the most important functions of a leader. You must coach, motivate, and manage to unleash the maximum potential of your sales team (and any other team, for that matter). Understanding this cadence helps both the salesperson to build their success plans and the sales leader to track progress against them and unleash the real potential of their sales teams.

Along the way, I will share wisdom, insights, and research from some of the top minds in professional sales and business today, many of whom have been guests on *The Selling Well* podcast that I host.

Let's get started on the path to learning to love selling well.

Part 1

CREATE YOUR SALES PLAYBOOK

Chapter 1

THE SALES PLAYBOOK

As entrepreneurs and salespeople, we need to understand only four things to convert our core business capability—meaning, whatever product or service we offer—into revenue:

- **Value Proposition**
- **Territory Management**
- **Demand Generation**
- **Sales Execution**

Collectively, these four components make up your sales program or, as we call it, your sales playbook. The details of your sales playbook will change, but the structure remains the same whether you are a small or medium business or a global software company.

The sales playbook is your starting point for every year and every quarter. Think of it as the road map for a long road trip you are about to take with your family. You review it before setting out on your voyage and check back in continuously to ensure you are on track and still going in the right direction. You might even discover some new information along the way and alter your route to improve your trip; everything goes into the playbook.

But most entrepreneurs and sales teams don't have a plan; instead, they respond to customer-driven demand and customer issues, hoping that *keeping busy* might lead them to their sales goals and business objectives.

It won't.

Small- and medium-sized businesses constantly struggle with revenue growth, sometimes for decades. They usually rely on the founder or one or two top performers, while the rest of the salespeople struggle with below-average performance.

Large enterprises constantly struggle with acquiring new customers and onboarding new sales hires successfully.

Building a sales playbook for your team enables everyone to understand how you expect the company to compete and win in your chosen markets and what activities you expect of the salespeople to be successful.

The sales playbook also applies at the salesperson's level. It's their plan to maximize revenue growth within their specific sales territory.

This chapter will provide an overview of the core elements of the IN THE FUNNEL Sales Playbook so you can start to think about what the playbook will look like for your business.

SALES PLAYBOOK

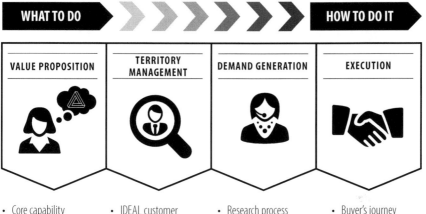

WHAT TO DO >>>>> **HOW TO DO IT**

VALUE PROPOSITION	TERRITORY MANAGEMENT	DEMAND GENERATION	EXECUTION
• Core capability • Desired business outcomes we provide clients • Competitive differentiation	• IDEAL customer profile • Buyer personas • Current client growth • New logo growth	• Research process • Lead engagement sequence • Call process strategy • Objection handling	• Buyer's journey • Sales process • Sales strategy • Sales funnel

Value Proposition

Your value proposition explains why prospects should work with you. It is the summary statement of how you expect to compete and win in your chosen marketplace. Regardless of the stage of a sales cycle (beginning, middle, or end), you will constantly be reiterating your value proposition to your prospects, so they know how and why you are the best choice to help them.

Unless you are in an unbelievably unique space, buyers generally have many options available to them. If you want to earn their time and attention, you need to understand precisely how you will respond when a buyer says, "I appreciate you reaching out to me, but we are delighted with our existing provider. Why should we consider you instead?"

The answer to that question is your value proposition (or value proposition statement). There are three things that you must capture and communicate well when crafting your value proposition statement for your business:

1. **Your core business capability**

   This answers the question: *What do you do?*

2. **The desired business outcome(s) that you provide customers**

   This answers the questions: *Why should someone engage you?* and *What will they get out of it?*

3. **Your competitive differentiation**

   This answers the question: *What is truly unique and different about you, given that customers have many other options in the marketplace?*

If you can answer these questions *and* resonate with your buyer, they may allow you to proceed to the next step of the buying process (and yes, I said *the buying process* instead of *the sales process* for a reason). More to come on the buyer's journey in Chapter 5.

If you cannot communicate your value proposition concisely and effectively, we are wasting their time (a cardinal sin in professional sales) and wasting yours.

Can you genuinely answer the question, "Why should your customers buy from you over anyone else?"

Be honest...chances are that your answer is *no* because this is surprisingly challenging, even for large, well-established organizations. Many sellers get used to responding to that question with marketing fluff extracted from the website or their marketing materials, things like:

- **We have been in business for ten years. (Nobody cares.)**
- **We have 125 employees. (Again, nobody cares.)**
- **We're one of the top sales training companies in North America. (That's our opinion, it's not a fact our prospects will believe.)**
- **Customers love our service-based culture. (Again, our opinion, not a fact.)**

Some of these statements are opinions, and a few are facts, but none is relevant to your prospect because they focus on *you* and not on *them*.

In professional sales, everything must be focused on how you can help your prospect achieve a desirable business outcome. It's always about them, not you.

Territory Management

Once you understand your value proposition, you must prioritize your efforts to pursue your target market.

Knowing your target market starts with identifying your Ideal Customer Profile (ICP). Answer these questions to clarify who you want as a customer:

- **What size customer is right for you? (small, medium, large)**
- **What industry are your best customers in?**
- **What business problems are they facing that you solve better than anyone else?**
- **How do they make decisions as a business?**

- Who are the specific people/roles within the organization that buy your offering?
- And perhaps *most importantly*, how big a customer will they be for you and your business?

There are only two sources of new sales opportunities for your business:

Current Customers: You can upsell or cross-sell other solutions if you have multiple ways of helping existing customers. This is also known as the growing "share of wallet."

New Customers: A *new logo* is a company within your target market that has not yet purchased from you. Once you sell to them, they will be a "new logo" you can post on your website, hence the term.

Prioritize your pursuit of each of these groups to create qualified sales opportunities with potential customers that resemble your Ideal Customer Profile. When defining your ICP, you need to identify all the attributes of the perfect customer for you and your business. If this appears to be a challenging exercise, look to your current customer roster to reveal which customers you are most happy to be working with today.

 Pro Tip: Set up a meeting with the key buyers among your top twenty customers. Interview them on why they work with you and what makes your company better than their other options in the marketplace. Existing customers will help you understand exactly why they originally chose you and continue to work with you. You might be surprised at what they truly value about working with you and your firm.

Most salespeople are highly reactive. They respond to *any* prospects who have an interest in them. This is the approach I took to dating in high school. I was so surprised that *anyone* liked me that I was more than happy to go out with whoever showed interest in me (truth be told...it was a pretty small list!). Only after I started learning about what attributes I was looking for in a partner did I proactively seek out those qualities. I apologize to the unfortunate young women who helped me understand this tough lesson in my youth!

In the same way, we need to be smarter with our sales territories. Time is the only limiting resource in professional sales. We must focus our activities on prospects who will significantly impact our sales goals and sell to our Ideal Customer Profiles.

Efficiency matters. Productivity matters. We need to hit our goals and objectives yearly so we cannot waste our time floundering around and selling to the wrong prospects.

 Pro Tip: It's just as difficult and time-consuming to sell to the wrong ICP as it is to sell to the right one.

Demand Generation

Once you know *why* someone should buy from you (value proposition) and have determined *who* should buy from you (ICP), you next need to engage with them.

Successful salespeople generate demand for the products and services they sell. This is what we used to call cold-calling. For decades, demand generation has been the X factor of professional sales. While most salespeople know what needs to be done, they do not know how to do it consistently or successfully. As a result, they constantly struggle to fill the top of their sales funnel.

Most salespeople are comfortable responding to inbound leads or working with current customers. Demand generation requires a salesperson to reach out to someone new and potentially face rejection. At the core, this is why most salespeople today avoid this function...after all, none of us likes the prospect of being rejected. It becomes a vicious cycle: salespeople avoid prospecting and, as a result, are not good at doing it, reinforcing their desire to avoid it. As a result, most "salespeople" today are account managers, leading to low growth.

The good news for salespeople who dread the "cold" aspect of demand generation is that sales technologies and social media have made this function much "warmer." We can easily learn about the prospects we are contacting before speaking with them. In addition, the sales tech stack (all the technologies you will leverage) will help you have the right conversation with the right buyer at the right time. More on this in Chapter 6, "The Sales Tech Stack."

Sales Execution

Once we create a qualified sales opportunity, we must sell better than the competitors to win the deal. Selling well matters. *How* you sell matters more than *what* you sell. The salesperson's skill makes the ultimate difference in who wins the deal.

Let's start by defining what sales isn't:

- cajoling or tricking a buyer into engaging with you
- pitching at a buyer like a talking brochure
- selling someone something their business does not need
- pressuring buyers at the quarter's end because you are desperate to hit your sales targets

Pro Tip: Professional selling: helping a customer solve a significant problem in a way that is mutually beneficial to them and you.

Sales is a profession, and we must behave with ethics and standards as salespeople. First and foremost, we must do what benefits the customer and always act honestly, openly, and forthrightly. This sounds unbelievably simple, but it is easy to forget when salespeople are under stress and feel pressure to deliver on sales goals.

To be a company that sells well *and* does so with integrity, we need to think about the following as part of sales execution:

1. **How we qualify leads**
   - Does this lead fit our ICP?
   - Do they have a need for our solution?
   - Are we working with people who have the authority to buy?
2. **Our sales process**
   - What are the specific steps/stages we need to follow to complete a sale for our business? For each stage, we need to understand:
     - Objectives of that stage
     - Sales activities we should complete at that stage
     - Exit criteria that help us understand when we have completed the stage
   - What value and insights can we provide our customers that differentiate us in the market?
   - How do we engage the prospect to work with us to determine the impact and value of our solution on their business?
   - Discovery is the most critical phase of the sales process because this is where we learn about *them*.

3. **The buyer's journey**
   - What process does our prospect go through to identify their need, identify potential solutions, and ultimately decide on a vendor?
   - How do prospects build a financial business case that will cost-justify making this purchase?
   - How do they get consensus among a group of buyers to decide?

4. **Sales strategy**
   - How do we navigate the various buyers who will influence the decision to purchase our solution?
   - How do we determine what is important to each buyer? How do we provide to them?
   - How do we earn their trust and confidence?

5. **Sales funnel**
   - What volume of sales activities is required to achieve sales results?
   - The final component of the sales playbook, execution, is where we convert a qualified opportunity into a sale for our business by selling well.

In the words of serial entrepreneur and investor Pino Iannetti:

> *It's always the same in every business and industry that I invest in. The core elements of the ITF Sales Playbook apply. I am shocked at how consistently this applies, whether it's a business-to-business enterprise software company selling into large banks or a life-sciences company selling into health care. The core elements of the ITF Sales Playbook apply. I have applied it to multiple companies that I invest in, both large and small, and the framework works every time.*

CHAPTER SUMMARY

- *How* you sell is at least as important as *what* you sell.
- Professional sales is about helping clients achieve a meaningful business outcome that benefits them and you.
- Sales is a profession, so we always act with integrity.
- To convert your core business capability into revenue, you need to build your sales playbook for your business and then execute it.

The core elements of the sales playbook include:

- your *value proposition* to your market
- your plan to prioritize the pursuit of your *target market*
- *demand-generation* activities to create awareness, attention, and need for your product and services
- how you execute your sales playbook by leveraging a *sales process* and *strategy* aligning with your buyer's journey

Chapter 2

VALUE PROPOSITION

I took my seat at the head of the boardroom table at the offices of a company we'll call Teamscape (to protect the innocent). They were a relatively small outfit of about twenty-five people, and their office was a lovely space with a good view of the park next door. Founders Doug and Cindy (again, not their real names) had built a fantastic business, but growth had slowed in recent years, so they reached out to IN THE FUNNEL for help. The company had a software application that helped utility companies manage their field staff—a unique product with few competitors, from what I understood in our initial phone conversation.

"OK, let's get started," I told the co-founders as I began a role-play exercise. "I am a buyer at a utility company in your target market... why should I talk to you?"

Cindy picked up a small remote from the table and clicked on the projector as Doug woke up his laptop. I saw a PowerPoint presentation on the screen with the Teamscape logo and the title "Company History." I swallowed hard as I took the next sip of my black coffee and thought, *Here we go.*

What followed was no surprise because it's the same thing I see over and over with entrepreneurs and salespeople. As the slideshow progressed, the information became less and less relevant to me, the pretend target customer for Teamscape.

> *"The company was founded in 2010..."*
> *"We have a combined fifty-six years of experience in the utility industry..."*
> *"Our technology uses the latest web-based security protocols..."*
> *"Voted Best Place to Work in 2019, 2021."*
> *"The features of our software are the best in the industry..."*

Doug and Cindy were committing a cardinal sin in professional sales: the presentation was a *pitch* at me, acting as their buyer *(and* doing a great job of it if you're reading this, Francis Ford Coppola).

The pitch was all about them and not about how to help me, their prospect.

Think of your worst first date ever; the person spoke about themselves all evening and was uninterested in *you.*

To make matters worse, most sales presentations do not communicate the company's value proposition from the potential customer's perspective. Most salespeople would rather drone on about features, functions, technology, or even the head count of the team when all the potential customer cares about is, "How can you help me achieve my business objectives or solve a significant business problem for me?"

Of course, before you can articulate this answer to your potential customers, you need to figure out the value proposition of your business and ensure that your entire team has it embedded in all external communications.

I can't stress this enough: the first thing any professional salesperson in your company needs to know prior to being exposed to any customers or prospects is your company's value proposition.

 Pro Tip: *"If you can't explain it simply, you don't understand it well enough."* —Albert Einstein

---

Your value proposition explains why a client or prospect should do business with your company. It concisely explains your core business strategy, i.e., how you expect to compete and win in your marketplace. It must answer these three questions:

- What do you do?
- What problem does that solve for your customers?
- How are you unique and different given the customer's other options in the marketplace to solve the same problem?

This may sound deceptively simple, but unless you have discussed this topic extensively with your team, chances are your company execs, and down to your newest sales hires, are articulating your value proposition *very* differently. This problem will not only lead to inconsistencies around how your team is presenting your offerings but also decrease your chances of winning new business.

Brevity and clarity are essential when crafting your value proposition. This can best be proven by the Forgetting Curve, developed by Hermann Ebbinghaus back in 1885. He developed a formula for understanding how quickly humans start losing the memory of learned knowledge over time. Ebbinghaus found that unless someone took the time to actively review new material, a typical person would halve their memory on learned knowledge in a matter of hours to weeks, inevitably forgetting it.[8]

So if we want any chance of really standing out to a prospect, we need an amazingly crisp and concise value proposition.

How often has it happened that you meet someone at a dinner party and ask them, "Hey, what do you do for a living?" only to have them ramble on for a few minutes about everything and the kitchen sink? When your partner asks you about what your new friend does later in the evening, you reply, "I have no idea!"

I felt this when Doug and Cindy reached the end of their extensive PowerPoint deck about Teamscape.

You may remember some vague points at best, but the impression will only be memorable if their value proposition has been refined. You will likely only remember something obscure about their business, such as the location, years in existence, or how they came up with the brand name, but nothing that will necessarily make you want to become a customer.

When workshopping your value proposition with your team, the idea is to nail down the points you want a prospective customer to *retain* because those are the points that matter most. If the impression you leave during a casual party conversation is subpar, it will undoubtedly be just as vague to a prospect on a sales call.

Think of your value proposition as a "three-legged stool" that describes these three tenets of your business:

- **Core Capability:** What do you do or offer (service or product)?
- **Desired Business Outcomes:** Why should they care about what you do?
- **Competitive Differentiation:** What is unique, different, and better about your offerings versus the other options they have in the marketplace?

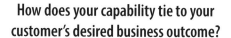

How does your capability tie to your customer's desired business outcome?

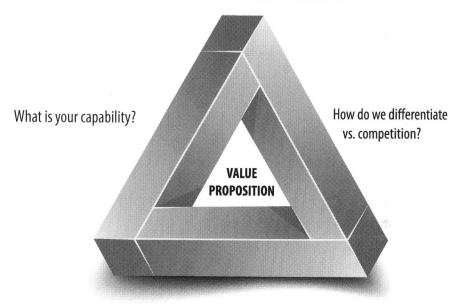

What is your capability?

How do we differentiate vs. competition?

VALUE PROPOSITION

Let's go over these one by one.

Core Capability

Your core capability is a sentence or two that highlights what your business does. When establishing this, please drop the acronyms, buzzwords, and techno-gab and make sure this description is understandable for anyone, even if they aren't from your industry. Just say it in plain English that a grade-nine student could understand: What do you do? As Michael Scott from *The Office* said, "Why don't you explain this to me like I'm five?"

The easiest way to illustrate a succinct core capability statement is to share my own from IN THE FUNNEL Sales Consulting:

> *We are a group of sales coaches that help companies sell better.*

No fancy buzzwords or catchphrases—just simple, direct language. Most prospects will only remember key bullet points about your business. People make decisions based on simple facts. So, explain what you do in language that even Michael Scott will understand!

Notice that even in the core capability statement, we have taken the customer's point of view: "help companies sell better" versus "provide sales training."

Desired Business Outcomes

Next, you must tie your core capability to a desired business outcome for your prospect. They need to know how you can help them.

Your core capability answers what you do, but your desired business outcome highlights why they should care about what you do from their perspective.

At the highest level, your prospects (and all profit-driven businesses, for that matter) have only three desired business outcomes. They want to:

- **increase revenue**
- **reduce costs and expenses**
- **reduce risk in the business**

These things matter because they are the critical levers for increasing the actual value of any business. These outcomes are what *they* care about, which is all that matters.

If your core capability can be directly tied to one or all of your customers' desired outcomes, there's a good chance that your prospect will see value in working with you to get a positive result.

The desired business outcome phrasing must encapsulate the prospect's perspective to get them to see that value. I find it effective to use the framing of "Customers typically engage us when..." in order to position your previous wins with other customers top of mind with the new prospective customer.

Going back to the IN THE FUNNEL example, we articulate our desired business outcomes as follows:

> *Customers typically engage us when they want to accelerate profitable revenue growth or differentiate in their market by how well they sell.*

This framing is like putting a mirror up before your prospect's face. They will immediately start to consider whether they have one (or several) of these problems or desires and what it would feel like to achieve this business outcome.

One of the most effective approaches I have seen was from one of my SaaS software customers. They pulled up a slide early in their brief value-proposition presentation showing five problems their typical customers had before working with them. They then asked the prospect which of these resonated with them most. Not only is this an effective way to articulate the desired business outcomes you help customers achieve, but it also helps guide the remainder of the discussion around the right problems instead of making broad assumptions that all prospects are struggling with the same issues.

Competitive Differentiation

Here is the kicker: you next need to establish your competitive differentiation.

Given the customer's other options, what makes you unique and different in your market?

To round off the last part of your three-legged value proposition, you must highlight why your company (or the solution you provide) is *better than anything else* available to your prospect. The one caveat is that you aren't only competing against other solution providers but often competing against the most dangerous competitor of all: inertia. The dreaded "do nothing" option has killed many deals, and the problem worsens.

According to Matthew Dixon and Ted McKenna, authors of *The JOLT Effect*, "Forty to sixty percent of deals today end up stalled in 'no decision' limbo. To be clear, these are customers who go through the entire sales process—consuming valuable seller time and organizational resources, perhaps even engaging in extended pilots or proof-of-concept trials—only to end up not crossing the finish line."[9]

For her excellent book *Relevant Selling*, Jaynie L. Smith polled three thousand mid-sized businesses and found that 90 percent had "No clue on how to articulate the competitive advantages of their offerings."[10] Let's ensure you are not one of these companies in her next poll.

According to Smith, the factors that make up your competitive differentiation must be:

- fact-based
- relevant to your customers
- directly comparable to your competitors

Many companies I've trained tend to struggle with this last part of the value proposition and commonly lean on generic "motherhood and apple pie statements" instead of fact-based data points describing what makes them truly unique and different. Saying you have "the best service" in your given industry is not a fact; it's an opinion. How do you prove that? According to whom?

Generic statements don't answer any questions for the prospect, often resulting in them leaving the meeting with even more questions. Similarly, saying you've been in business for fifteen years may be a fact, but it's utterly irrelevant to your customers unless you clarify how that experience helps them today.

For example, we trained a fantastic sales team in the industrial refrigeration industry, CIMCO Refrigeration. CIMCO has been in business for over one hundred years (yes, awe-inspiring). However, when we refined their value proposition, we explained why that experience specifically helped their customers:

CIMCO Refrigeration Value Proposition: Competitive Differentiation
Customers tell us we are unique and different in this market because of our global size, scale, and experience. They appreciate the best practices and innovations we bring to their environments, learned from building ½ the rinks in the world and completing $ 1.6 B in projects last decade. 95.6 percent of our 7,000 customers continue to work with us year after year.

When workshopping your competitive differentiation, step away from qualitative points and zero in on quantitative aspects of what makes your company truly unique and better. Start digging into impressive numbers or metrics that you can leverage or competitive differences that make you memorable versus your prospect's other options in the market. And remember, don't forget the "do-nothing" competitor!

Getting back to Doug and Cindy, can you imagine how much more effective their presentation would have been had they cited a study from a third party showing that their software increases the daily productivity of a service person in the field by 15 percent in the first twelve months? This is powerful stuff that cuts through the noise with prospects.

The bottom line is that if you cannot clearly and concisely articulate why you are better, more unique, or different than your competitors, then you won't win. If your buyer believes that multiple competitors are more or less the same with limited competitive differentiation, then the only way to differentiate is price. This is how certain industries become commoditized, and this is the last place that entrepreneurs and salespeople want to end up when competing for business.

At IN THE FUNNEL, we are playing in a very crowded space with many other sales training companies, so it is even more crucial for us to articulate what sets us apart from the different options available in the market. Here is how we view our competitive differentiation:

> *Our customers tell us that we are unique and different in our space for three reasons: 1) We provide our customers with access to our online learning portal, the IN THE FUNNEL Sales Academy, so they can continue learning at their time and pace after the training events. 2) All workshops are taught by sales leaders who have run a material sales organization in the recent past. We are sales practitioners,*

not theorists. 3) We have offered a FULL 100 percent money-back guarantee to each of the thousands of entrepreneurs, sales leaders, and salespeople who have taken our workshops, and NOBODY (not a single one) has ever asked for it.

Implementation

Now comes the most challenging part: How do you implement this new value-proposition messaging approach into your company and make it uniform for your sales and marketing teams? The first thing to know is that it takes time. It will not happen in a five- or ten-minute meeting; working through and refining your value proposition with your executive and sales teams can take days.

Every team member needs to learn your entire value-proposition statement and let it soak deep into every fiber of their being. Your value proposition is to your sales process what the foundation is to a house—it underpins everything.

To tie it all together, here is the full IN THE FUNNEL Value Proposition Statement:

> *At IN THE FUNNEL, we are a group of sales coaches that help companies sell better.*

Customers typically engage us when they want to accelerate profitable revenue growth or differentiate in their market by how well they sell.

Customers tell us that we are unique and different in our space for three reasons:

- We provide our customers with access to our online learning portal, the IN THE FUNNEL Sales Academy, so they can continue their learning on their own time and at their own pace.
- All workshops are taught by sales leaders who have run a material sales organization in the recent past. We are sales practitioners, not theorists, and bring our experience to every workshop.
- We have offered a full money-back guarantee to each and every student we have ever taught and NOT ONE has ever asked for it.

Of course, when we must keep this ultra-brief (twenty seconds on a demand-generation call), we select one or two bullet points from each value proposition component.

Here's an exercise to run with the team to develop the first draft of your Value Proposition Statement.

Exercise: Create the value proposition for your business.

1. Whiteboard multiple potential phrases for each element of the value proposition.

Remember, the concept of a whiteboard is that you put lots of ideas on the whiteboard, without judging, rebutting, or editing them. More options are better than fewer at this stage.

2. **Short-list the top two or three phrases for each element of the value proposition.**

    This is where judgment and editing come into play.

3. **Put them all together in this order:**

    a. What we do
    b. Desired business outcomes that we provide customers
        i. Why do customers engage us?
    c. Competitive differentiation
        ii. What makes us unique and different?

As this messaging needs to be uniform for the whole company, get various opinions from the entire team and find great examples of what you do, what type of customers engage with you, and why you're the best solution on the market.

 To download a tool that will help you to build your value proposition statement, go here and use the password "thesellingwell":
https://www.inthefunnel.com/ltls-sales-tools

As you workshop your value proposition, beware of a couple of common pitfalls:

1. **For your core capability and desired business outcome, you might find yourself and your team caught in the weeds with too many options to narrow down.**
2. **The opposite might happen with competitive differentiation, which leaves you struggling to determine fact-based reasons that you are unique.**

If you need help narrowing things down, find the top two or three phrases and terms consistent across the team and use those as the starting point. This is not a five-to-ten-minute exercise because, off the top of your head, it might be easy to come up with any number of issues, but refining it to the relevant top three is what will make this value proposition pop. Just take the time to refine!

 Pro Tip: One of the best places to start to get additional ideas for both (1) the desired business outcomes you provide and (2) competitive differentiation, is your best customers. Your customers are smart and there are logical reasons they bought from you—so find them out and use them when explaining to the next prospect why they should buy from you.

If this seems like a lot of work as a starting point to build your sales playbook, it is. However, it's worth putting the time and effort into getting this right. Once you have crafted an effective value proposition for your business, you will leverage it in all the following places:

- your website
- social media sites
- all other marketing materials
- every demand-generation reach-out
- all proposals and presentations
- almost every time you explain your business to anyone

See? It's that important.

CHAPTER SUMMARY

- Understanding your value proposition to the market is the starting point in building your sales playbook.
- There are three components to your value proposition:
    - **Core Capability**—what you do
    - **Desired Outcomes**—why prospects should care about what you do
    - **Competitive Differentiation**—what makes you unique and different in your marketplace
        - fact-based
        - relevant to the customer
        - relative to the competitors
- Your value proposition statement must be concise if you want your prospects to retain it.
- Your value proposition articulates your core business strategy and will be the basis of all of your marketing.

Chapter 3

TERRITORY MANAGEMENT

Royston and I sat at the corner table in my favorite café in downtown Toronto. He is a longtime friend who runs a successful software business helping financial institutions with social media monitoring and is a great overall guy. We often meet to share the latest wins and challenges with our companies while catching up about life, family, and anything else that comes to mind. I immediately noticed that Royston seemed a little less energetic than usual.

"How's business at SeeMe.com?" I asked.

"It's crazy, Mark. We have this huge opportunity with a new health care provider in the northeast. I've been grinding hard to close the deal... burning the candle at both ends."

"Health care provider?" I asked. "I thought SeeMe.com was exclusively a financial services player."

"Well...this health care provider called me out of the blue, and it could be a huge opportunity," Royston said. "It could be five times the size of a normal project for us, but the team is nervous that the margins are much thinner and there are some potential land mines we might not know about. But it could be massive for us."

I paused before I dove in further. I know from previous coffee sessions that Royston has amazing financial services customers with SeeMe.com. He has built a tremendous reputation and an extremely profitable business focusing on the big-bank market in North America. Banks buy tested and proven solutions that other banks have already purchased, and SeeMe.com has top-tier, blue-chip banks as existing customers.

However, I have seen this type of issue many times before—companies get "shiny object syndrome" when a new potential customer approaches them. It becomes a disaster when they pursue this type of sales lead that is outside of their core competency.

As entrepreneurs or salespeople, many of us can get excited by any new or exciting opportunities. I do it in my own business! By no means am I saying every entrepreneur, business owner, or CEO should "stay in their lane" because new opportunities can often be transformative. I am saying that it's important to strategically define what type of customers your business wants and put as much energy as possible into identifying and pursuing customers that fit this profile.

To go back to basics: your objective in professional sales is to maximize revenue within the sales territories that you are responsible for. Once comfortable with a value proposition that resonates within your target market, you must prioritize pursuing that target market. This is called territory management, which is much more strategic than most think.

Your goal is to create new sales opportunities and then win them. So, the real questions you must ask yourself are, "What type of sales do

I *want,* and which type of sales can I *win*?" This means focusing your time and attention on the following:

- the current customers that have the most upside sales potential for you
- new customers that you most *want* to win
- new customers that you actually *can* win

TERRITORY MANAGEMENT

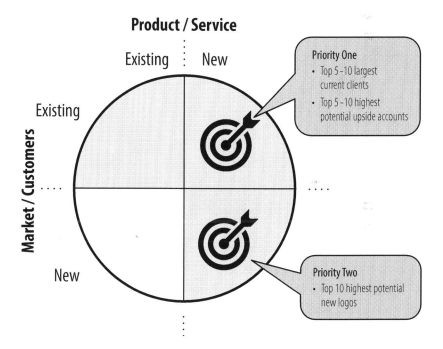

Product / Service

Existing : New

Market / Customers

Existing

New

Priority One
- Top 5–10 largest current clients
- Top 5–10 highest potential upside accounts

Priority Two
- Top 10 highest potential new logos

Think back to your Ideal Customer Profile (ICP), defined in the target market section of Chapter 1. Before you go out and try to grow the business or your sales territory, you must be clear on what kind of business the company wants to win!

Many salespeople think any sales opportunity is a good sales opportunity. It's not. How often have you chased a sales opportunity that is not a good fit for your business? How much valuable selling time have you or your team wasted on a deal that came inbound, only to realize it was too large or too complex and that you had no realistic chance of winning it?

How often have you pursued a sales opportunity and wasted countless resource hours, only to be told at the eleventh hour that you have lost because you do not have reference customers that look precisely like the prospect you are selling to? How many hours have you wasted filling out thick RFPs (requests for proposals) on opportunities from prospects that were never going to buy from a company your size? This is exactly the issue that Royston and SeeMe.com would inevitably face when they chased the deal with the health care provider.

 Pro Tip: If your company did not help the prospect write the RFP and tailor it to your strengths, you probably won't win it.

Don't feel bad—we have all fallen victim to chasing these low-probability sales cycles. Just because a buyer engages with you and could buy your offering doesn't mean they will. So many businesses today employ what I call the "spray and pray" approach to going to market with their products or services. They *spray* a message out there and *pray* that it resonates with someone willing to open their wallet and place an order.

A lack of clarity on the ICP is one of the most significant issues we see in sales today.

Exercise: Define and document your Ideal Customer Profile (ICP).

You already know your best customers because you're working with them now. The critical question is, *why?* Which customers do you like working with most and why? Which customers like working with you most and why?

Some existing customers are less attractive and profitable to your firm because of how they purchase or how they work with vendors or even their values as a company. As you create your ICP, consider all these dynamics to understand what success looks like for new customer acquisition.

Step 1—Identify your top ten to twenty customers.
Step 2—Build out a short profile on these customers, including:
- industry
- size (revenue and employees)
- business problem they have that your solution solves
- annual revenue/profit to your firm
- state of their business: growing or declining
- their company culture and values
- customer satisfaction—how happy they are working with you
- their buying process
- which roles/people influence the decision
- how they purchase your services
  - i.e., formal (RFP) or informal process
  - length of the sales cycle
- whom you compete with
  - how/why you win the sale

Back to Royston. Even though he was excited about the potential revenue from the vast health care provider, they were not going to win that deal. A large enterprise like a health care provider is highly risk-averse, and they only engage suppliers with many customers that look exactly like them. So eventually, someone was going to ask Royston which other large-scale health providers he was working with right now, and when Royston said, "None," he would lose. All that time spent jumping through hoops to respond would be wasted.

You might ask yourself, "Why did the health care provider reach out to SeeMe.com at all?" The answer is that they wanted multiple proposals to validate their original choice for the vendor. They will need to justify to their bosses and internal decision-makers that they surveyed the market to ensure the vendor they wanted to work with provided a (somewhat) market-competitive price.

So, this sales effort benefits the prospect for administrative purposes but is a complete waste of time for SeeMe.com—although Royston doesn't know that.

We all have limited time and resources, so you must focus your sales efforts on a specific target market where:

- **You can find the types of deals you want.**
- **You have the highest potential to win those deals.**
- **You can win those deals in the shortest time frame possible.**

Now, think about how you generate new sales opportunities that resemble your ICP. As a reminder, you have only two sources for these: current customers (if you have additional products and services that you can sell to your base of customers) or new customers.

Selling to Current (Existing) Customers
The process of selling to current customers is often referred to as a "growing share of wallets." Many successful businesses apply a

land-and-expand strategy by starting with one product or service and then driving additional revenue from that same account. Growing your share of wallet is the easiest way to accelerate revenue growth for your business or sales territory for several reasons:

- **The customer already knows and trusts you and your company.**
- **Your value proposition resonates with them because they have already purchased from you.**
- **You have access to the key decision-making buyers in the account.**
- **You have already successfully contracted with the customer, so no contract deal-breakers exist.**

Selling to your existing base of customers is the logical, best initial use of sales capacity for any salesperson managing a territory. So, as you might expect, this is where many salespeople spend most of their time.

Selling to existing customers is also easier because of their own confirmation biases.

Daniel Kahneman initially identified this concept in his *New York Times* bestseller *Thinking, Fast and Slow.* Robert Cialdini simplifies the concept as "Our obsessive desire to be (and appear) consistent with what we have already done. Once we have made a choice or taken a stand, we will encounter personal and interpersonal pressures to behave consistently with that commitment. Those pressures will cause us to respond in ways that justify our earlier decision."[11]

Focusing on growing within our base of existing customers is productive and efficient. However, the one nasty side effect is that for some salespeople, this becomes the only place they spend their time.

In my experience, about 80 percent of professional salespeople today are only account managers: they manage only current customers and do not pursue any new business. They work with and grow their existing base of customers and will even respond well to inbound leads, but they do little or no demand generation to create sales opportunities. This avoidance of doing demand generation to new prospects will limit their ability to achieve consistent success.

Let's use an example of a salesperson with one hundred accounts or current customers. She needs to prioritize her sales and account management efforts within that base. Her working assumption for territory management is based on two key factors:

- Her firm can sell a customer multiple products or services.
- The *Pareto Principle* (also known as the 80/20 rule) means that roughly 80 percent of the revenue will come from the top 20 percent of customers.

How should she prioritize her time spent with accounts to maximize revenue growth?

Priority One: largest customers. She must treat her most significant customers *as* her largest and most important customers and spend a proportionate amount of time with them.

Priority Two: customers with the most growth potential. These customers have a significant potential need for your products or services but have yet to engage you to the maximum extent. Perhaps they are using a competitor or doing some equivalent work with an in-house team.

The ITF Health Check Meeting
One of the critical challenges is that salespeople often have no process or strategy for driving new sales from existing customers apart

from waiting for a customer contact to engage them and ask for it. Salespeople like to drop in for fly-by meetings with customers or take them out for lunch or coffee, but these unstructured, ad-hoc events rarely create new qualified sales opportunities. At best, they keep you front of mind when the customer has a need for your offerings. So, how can you proactively create sales opportunities from your existing base of customers in the next thirty to sixty days?

We have developed a straightforward and effective way to generate sales opportunities from your existing customer base called the ITF Health Check Meeting. If there's one immediate action you should take after (or while) reading this book, it's to reach out to your Priority One and Priority Two current customers using the following email template. This sample uses our hypothetical customer Radia Corporation and our contact Stefani.

Hi Stefani,

I hope all is well with you and yours.

As a matter of course, we like to have a semi-annual health check meeting for our most important customers.

The objective of this meeting is simple: we want to understand how we are performing as a partner with Radia Corporation and gather any feedback on how to be more effective at helping you drive your desired results.

The agenda is simple (please feel free to add to this):

1. *How are we doing as a provider?*
2. *What's new with Radia Corporation?*
   - *Priority business objectives for the coming twelve months.*
   - *How are you progressing against them?*
3. *What's new with IN THE FUNNEL?*
   - *Priority objectives for the next twelve months.*
   - *Insights on the industry and market.*
4. *Next steps.*

 Download a sample of our ITF Health Check Agenda here: https://www.inthefunnel.com/ltls-sales-tools
Password: thesellingwell

This simple strategy has been a fantastic trigger for improving relationships with existing customers and quickly creating new sales pipelines from those customers.

Believe it or not, customers *want* to provide feedback to improve your relationship. However, feedback is often difficult to deliver on the spot in a lunch or coffee meeting. Customers need to be prompted and given time to think to provide helpful feedback. They will think about the value that you have provided; when they speak it aloud in the meeting, they'll reinforce that value and imprint it within their mind even further, in the same way positive self-talk helps our mindset.

The health check meeting is a great opportunity to strengthen existing relationships with that customer and expand your relationships within the account. More importantly, it's about learning what's going on with them. Often, your contacts will not be inclined to invite their teammates or bosses to another lunch or coffee with a salesperson because they are careful not to waste their time. They may, however, be more open to inviting a boss or co-worker to the meeting if there is a structured agenda. In your follow-up to the health check meeting invitation, you can suggest this by saying something like, "Hey Stefani, my boss Sandra wanted to join this meeting to get feedback from Radia Corporation. Is there anyone else on your end that you would like to invite?"

 Pro Tip: Running a health check meeting with your most important customers is even more important if you fear there is some negative feedback coming.

A few of our customers have expressed concerns about establishing these meetings for fear that some feedback would be negative. Salespeople are often afraid of what they might hear regarding how the customer has perceived their performance, but the truth is that even if the feedback is negative, it can result in positive outcomes. If you receive less than complimentary feedback, you can reply with, "Thank you so much for the honesty and the feedback, Stefani. I am so glad that I asked you to this meeting. Please tell me more, and I will plan to come back within a couple of days with a detailed plan for resolving these issues."

Very few vendors or suppliers *ever* ask for feedback from their customers, so by doing so, you have shown that your company cares and that you value the relationship. If you can use the feedback to improve your offerings or potentially find new ways of helping your customer—which results in new revenue for your business—all the better!

The feedback I have received on this health check approach has been universally positive, both from the sales teams we train and their customers. These meetings have better outcomes the more the *customer* speaks.

> When they give feedback, your sales team should use the ITF Sales Multipliers: what, why, how, and please tell me more. This will lead to a more detailed discovery and a better outcome for the meeting.

Selling to New Customers (New Logos)

After focusing on growing share of wallet from existing customers, we need to target new customers.

How do you create demand from new logos or those companies who appear to fit your ICP but have yet to purchase products or services from you? The paradox of choice means that the more options for potential customers, the more anxiety we feel, which often leads to making less progress. That is why we ask all salespeople to build their territory game plan at the beginning of the month and stick to it, using the adage "plan your work and work your plan." Identify the ten to twenty new logo targets you will initiate first contact with, and regularly track progress with your sales leader.

Selling to new customers is one of the most difficult things in professional sales and a crucial survival factor for entrepreneurs. Opening is the new closing in sales, meaning creating new sales cycles is almost as important as winning them.

The key to selling new logos is demand generation. This topic is so important that we dedicate a full chapter to it next.

For a simple tool to help with
your territory game plan, go to:
https://www.inthefunnel.com/ltls-sales-tools
Password: thesellingwell

CHAPTER SUMMARY

- Once you understand your company's value proposition to the market, you need to prioritize the pursuit of that market.
- Start by identifying your Ideal Customer Profile (ICP).
- Then create your territory game plan to create qualified sales opportunities of ICPs from:
  - existing customers
  - new clients
- Customers buy from specialists who have a proven track record selling to other customers who look exactly like them.

Chapter 4

DEMAND GENERATION

I was in the prime of my career. I was in professional sales, selling an industry-leading software solution to the financial industry, and every day, my inbox was overflowing with people who had filled out our online form requesting a meeting to discuss our software. Our business could barely keep up with the demand. Revenue was coming in faster than we could account for it, and the most significant decision we had to make daily was how much to increase our prices. Leads flowed like water, and every new opportunity was juicier than the last.

Then, I got a rude awakening.

It was all a dream.

While most normal people dream of flying through clouds like Superman or bungee jumping beside a beautiful blue waterfall in a rainforest, I was in my comfortable bed beside my lovely wife, Donna, dreaming about a stuffed sales funnel. Sad, isn't it?

As a professional salesperson, I yearned for a steady stream of prospects calling me to buy our products and services.

As I drove to the office that morning, I returned to the brutal reality of what awaited me. Potential customers were *not* contacting me in droves to buy our software product. Nobody was coming to us.

All of us would be delighted to have our marketing team provide so many inbound leads that all we would need to do every day is write orders for our products and services. The reality is that few companies are in this kind of privileged position. To be successful in business, we have to go out there and create demand.

Demand generation or prospecting is the biggest sales problem for most salespeople, even those in a mature, large company with a spectacular product.

Rob Madej is the founder and CEO of PureFacts Financial Solutions, a global leader in wealth management technology. They provide fees, billing, reporting, and insights to wealth management firms looking to maximize their assets under administration. They have some of the largest financial institutions in the world as long-term customers and have won multiple awards and accolades for being one of the world's top fintech and wealthtech companies.

They also had the even more prestigious honor of being the first IN THE FUNNEL customer ever, back in 2013.

When Rob brought us back in to help in 2021, one of the main reasons why was that he felt they needed a more well-defined sales strategy and plan to scale the business. They needed our sales playbook configured for their business. One of his specific concerns was growth from new business.

"Mark," he said, "we continue to grow this business well, and I am pleased about that. But I'm worried about how many new logos we add to the yearly roster. As you know, I love doing sales calls, and my team has only brought me into a handful of new prospect meetings in the last year. We need to change that and fast."

At that time, PureFacts had a marketing team and a couple of amazing salespeople in addition to Rob. But marketing was not providing enough (or any) inbound leads. This is the reality for a medium-sized business, even when the company has had a twenty-five-year run of amazing success in enterprise software, like PureFacts has.

A year later, we had built a sales development strategy and trained the team for PureFacts that was intentionally creating demand for PureFacts versus passively waiting for inbound leads. PureFacts was now engaging sixty new prospects per quarter to grow their business. Rob, a natural customer-first salesperson, was in front of these new prospects every week.

"If you build it, they will come" was the reality in the movie *Field of Dreams,* but it is the biggest fallacy in business.

Most of us don't get enough inbound leads from our marketing efforts to grow our businesses at the rates we want. We need to reach our target market and *create* demand for our offerings. This process is called outbound demand generation or prospecting. This is what they referred to as cold calling forty years ago—"cold" meant that you knew nothing about the prospect you were reaching out to back then. That's not the case today.

Demand generation targets new leads for your business. You "create demand" from prioritized prospects—the list of companies that fit your Ideal Customer Profile within your target market. The ability to do this well is a key success factor in professional sales today.

In my view, there are a couple of obvious reasons that proactive, outbound demand generation is the most avoided activity in sales. Most salespeople and entrepreneurs:

- do not know how to do it
- want to avoid the rejection that comes with it

Understandably, rejection makes people uncomfortable. It's not something that anyone who experiences normal human emotions ever comes to enjoy. Unfortunately, by design, demand generation sets us up for rejection because we are reaching out to people who:

- aren't expecting us to reach out
- don't think they need the product we are trying to introduce to them
- may not have a budget for whatever we are offering

Given these dynamics, we will face many nos on the way to a yes. Even though many of us logically understand that sales is a numbers game, none of us enjoys experiencing rejection. Hence, we need to prepare ourselves emotionally for this activity.

In the early 2000s, growth-oriented companies realized this gap and created a specialist sales model in which certain salespeople—sales development reps (SDRs)—focused exclusively on demand generation. Think of the sales team as an assembly line. Similarly to how someone in the General Motors plant puts on the fenders and passes the vehicle to the team installing the doors, an SDR generates an opportunity and then they pass it along to the account executive to take it from there. Aaron Ross and Marylou Tyler originally presented this concept in *Predictable Revenue.*[12]

The idea was that by focusing on demand generation exclusively, the SDRs would be better at it than general salespeople—it was optimization through specialization. Plus, it's difficult to focus on demand generation *and* execute on delivery and account management.

I agree with specializing in the demand-generation function, with one crucial caveat: having a team of SDRs will never absolve a professional salesperson of the need to generate their demand in addition to what the SDR team might drive. The bottom line is that if you are in professional sales, you *must* be capable of creating demand to succeed. Not only is this taking responsibility for your outcomes, but it is also one of the most effective ways to future-proof your career.

The Core Challenge of Demand Generation

When you initiate a demand-generation call, your immediate challenge is getting through the first ten to fifteen seconds and breaking down your prospect's aversion to speaking to salespeople. Sales stereotypes and hilariously bad demand generation have taught everyone to avoid salespeople (that's how I rationalize why nobody ever wants to talk with me at a cocktail party!).

Within seconds of a prospect taking our demand-generation call or reading your demand-generation email, they are asking themselves:

- **Why should I listen to this salesperson?**
- **Why should I care about what they are saying?**

THE CORE CHALLENGE OF DEMAND GENERATION

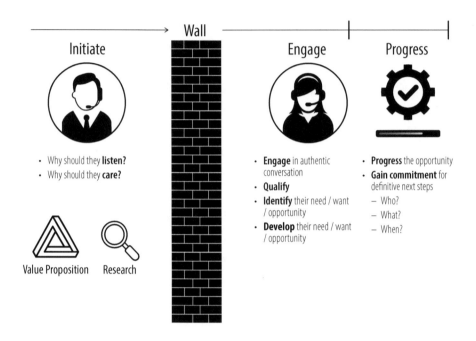

If you do not respond well to these critical questions, you will lose the prospect almost immediately. They will put up a "wall" either very directly by telling you they do not want to engage in the conversation or indirectly by giving inauthentic answers to your questions.

They often make up the answers that they think you need to hear to confirm that they don't need whatever you sell (this is the Canadian approach, as they are too nice to shut down the conversation). Typical answers about budget constraints or having too many other projects on the go are some of the most popular blocking mechanisms you will hear from disengaged prospects.

How do we knock down prospects' walls? This chapter shares IN THE FUNNEL's strategies, processes, and tools to address these core challenges head-on and enable you to succeed where many others fail.

We'll answer the following critical questions on demand generation:

- Whom do you reach out to?
- How should you prepare before reaching out?
- How do you get your first live conversation with a prospect?
- What exactly do you do during the first conversation?

Whom Do I Reach Out To?

Let's assume you have a solid list of one hundred prospects who fit your ICP. You must create a list of specific buyers within the ICP that you want to connect with. Most corporate buying decisions are made by groups within the prospect's organization working to get consensus on purchasing decisions, as opposed to one single individual. For example, when selling our sales training workshops to companies, we might be selling to:

1. founder/CEO
2. head of sales
3. head of human resources

So, there are three different roles or buyer personas that we can sell to.

The ITF Buyer Persona template is a valuable tool to help you understand your buyer personas, covering:

- What is the buyer accountable for in their organization?
- What pain points might the buyer be experiencing?
- What does a win look like for this buyer?
- What key trends are affecting their industry?

To download this template, go to:
https://www.inthefunnel.com/ltls-sales-tools
Password: thesellingwell

 Pro Tip: If you are selling to a buyer persona you don't understand yet, ask ChatGPT to help. For example, ask for a job description for a VP of human resources to get a list of things a "typical" head of HR is focused on.

How Should I Prepare Before Reaching Out?

Professional sales is about helping a customer solve a significant problem in a way that benefits them and you. It's not about pitching your product or service.

You need to connect with a prospect professionally and provide value and insight to help them run a better business or department. You earn the right to proceed to the next step by adding value, but you need to understand the prospect first to advance. The more profound level of understanding you have of the buyer and their business, the more meaningful contribution you may be able to make to them.

 Pro Tip: *"You can make more friends in two months by becoming genuinely interested in other people than you can in two years by trying to get others interested in you."*
—Dale Carnegie

At a minimum, before reaching out, you must research:

- the person (via LinkedIn)
- their company and industry (via LinkedIn, their website, 10-K reports, Google)
- unique point of interest (POI) that you can leverage to get them engaged on the call (learned via all channels noted above)

Why search for a unique point of interest (POI)?

You need to earn the right to converse with your prospect, and a point of interest shows them that you have done some homework before reaching out. This is an effective way to start building rapport and shows you care about them and not just your sales commissions. Nobody wants to speak with a salesperson who has "commission breath." Research and insights will add to your credibility and help you develop trust with the person. These are necessary steps to earn some of your prospect's time.

These days, there is no excuse for not conducting research before reaching out to a prospect. It is easier now than ever to learn about someone's career and company on LinkedIn, Google, articles, or via their website and public filings. While you can quickly find information about a business and someone's professional career, make sure you're keeping this research on a professional level and not jumping to their personal Facebook or Instagram page. There's a fine line

> between professional investigation and crossing into creepy country.
>
> Typically, this research on the POI should not take more than seven minutes. However, it should still be enough to start a compelling conversation to get your prospect to lower their wall of resistance and be open to a short discussion.

You must realize that when reaching out to a new prospect, they will naturally be skeptical of your intentions or what you are trying to achieve. Dr. Nick Morgan states, "Winning people's trust to get a commitment is an extremely sensitive activity: we humans are always asking why. We care about intent; trust for us is about knowing what their—the other person's or group's—intentions are."[13]

Doing your research will help differentiate you from the untrained, unsophisticated sellers pitching *at* prospects when they get them on the phone. I have found throughout my career that this simple strategy will very often trigger engagement, as the prospect will be slightly flattered that you have done work before picking up the phone to reach out. Believe it or not, it can also trigger (at some level) reciprocity, which, as Robert Cialdini said, is one of the "most potent weapons of influence around us."[14]

When performing demand generation, you must be clear on your high, medium, and low objectives for that call. The high-end objective is to provide value and insight to the prospect, and progress to the next step in your sales process. The minimum outcome from the call must be to learn more about the company and the prospect that you can use when reaching out again in the future.

For example:

- What are their business's top priorities, and what are issues/barriers to achieving them?
- How do they compete and win in their markets?
- What solutions are they using today that compete with what you provide?
- Who are the buyers influencing the decisions to use that solution?

There are a few more things to consider as you plan to reach out to a prospect:

- Plan your questions to drive the conversation forward from the start of the call.
- Ensure your prospect is speaking about 70 percent of the time during your conversation—this ensures you are digging deep enough and getting proper engagement from them.
- Stay authentic, be calm, confident, and curious, and ensure they know the conversation is about *them.*
- You cannot fake authentic curiosity, but you can cultivate it with great questions.

 To download a tool to help you craft amazing questions, go to:
https://www.inthefunnel.com/ltls-sales-tools
Password: thesellingwell

How Do You Get the First Live Conversation with a Prospect?
Once you've figured out who your prospect is, how do you connect with them for the first time? Do you reach out five times a day for a

week, once a day for thirty days in a row, or every day for a year? Do you leave a voicemail or not?

You must create a first-contact process (called the lead engagement sequence) to know when to start and finish working on a lead. If you don't leverage a defined engagement process, you can keep churning the same leads indefinitely with no plan or way to optimize your efforts. This activity becomes soul-destroying and kills your motivation.

So, how do you properly work a lead?

It's hard to believe, but in a professional environment, when approaching a potential buyer, statistics tell us it will take seven to twelve reach-outs (calls, emails, or a combination of both) before making the first contact. However, only 3 percent of salespeople even *try* connecting with a lead four times or more, which means there is a massive disconnect between the sales activity required for successful demand generation and the average rep's sales activity. The bottom line is we are all giving up too early, and the unfortunate side effect is that it makes us start to believe the false hype that demand generation doesn't work.

Connecting with a lead can be done in several ways, but the easiest way is to leverage a combination of calls/voicemails, emails, and reach-outs via LinkedIn. The actual number of reach-outs and the period over which they are completed is based on the size of your target market and the type of product or services you are selling. Generally speaking, the larger the target market, the shorter the lead engagement process. For example, our target market for IN THE FUNNEL is companies with sales teams between three and one hundred. This list is in the tens of thousands, so we reach out to one hundred per month using our sequence, and if they do not respond, we move on to the next list of one hundred.

Lead Engagement Sequence

There are thousands of potential lead engagement sequences that you can use leveraging multiple channels to reach out to your prospects. We suggest experimenting with multiple types and tracking the performance of what does and doesn't work. This testing never ends as strategies and tactics here become stale over time.

One of the lead engagement processes that we currently use is a three-week, eleven-touchpoint process, where we try to connect with the prospect four times in the first week, again four times in the second week, and three times in the third week, ending with a professional "breakup" voicemail and email.

LEAD ENGAGEMENT SEQUENCE

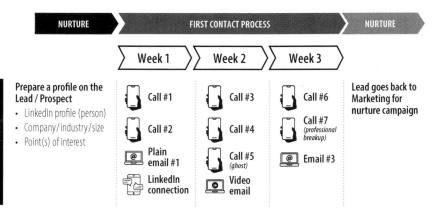

In the first week, you need to call twice, send an email, and send a LinkedIn connection with a message to the prospect. When you call, if you don't happen to get in touch, your voicemail should be less than twenty seconds and professionally convey a rehearsed message that explains your value proposition, references a point of interest on the person you're calling, and proposes a call-to-action for next steps. You can rehearse your demand-generation voicemail by calling your own phone and playing the message back while listening for:

Coherence: Does what you're saying make sense?
Pace: Are you speaking too quickly or too slowly?
Energy: Do you sound engaging or unhappy? Smile and stand up to improve how you sound.
Duration: How long is it? (Target fifteen to twenty seconds maximum)

Breaking through the spam filters of your customers and prospects gets more complex every day, and what worked in the past will not necessarily work in the future. One suggestion I always have for salespeople crafting their reach-outs is to make the first email to a new prospect text only (no images, videos, attachments, or links). This approach will improve your chances of getting through the spam filters and firewalls and set you up for better deliverability on future emails. As you conduct outreach, you must constantly track the delivery of your emails and open- and click-through rates to ensure they get through to the recipients. Virtually all marketing and sales automation technologies have this functionality built in.

In week two, you should aim to make three calls and send another email to the prospect. If you don't connect with the individual, two calls should be voicemails with a slightly altered message but a similar call-to-action: to book a meeting. The third call, however, should be a "ghost call." A ghost call is a call where you don't leave a voicemail. The ghost call is because you mustn't bombard your prospect with too many voicemails. Lastly, the email you sent in week two should also be brief with a clear call-to-action but reference a slightly different point of interest.

Now, some of you may start to think that a salesperson might be perceived as being too professionally persistent, but **remember:**

- In our sequence, we are leaving only two voicemails per week.
- If the lead responds to any of the emails with "I'm not interested," then we stop reaching out.

Now, we also need to consider how we wind down the sequence of reaching out to a lead.

In week three, if you haven't made the first contact, you should aim to make two last calls and one more email. However, the last call and email will be "professional breakup" messages.

The professional breakup is a surprisingly effective tactic that sounds somewhat counterintuitive but works well in practice. We didn't invent this approach but use it religiously in our process and with the sales teams we train. Although I'm no expert on human behavior, the concept is simple. When you keep calling a prospect, they often assume you will continue forever, so they see no urgency to respond, even if there is some interest in what you are presenting them with. Let's face it—most people in positions of influence making buying decisions are very busy. They are trying to prioritize their tasks, and if they don't see any urgency in getting back to you, it simply won't make it onto their list. However, something changes when you call to let them know this will be your last attempt to reach out:

- They understand that they will need to respond if they have a need.
- They understand that your time is valuable also and that you intend to engage only with those who have a need.

A critical aspect of the professional breakup is that your message is happy, pleasant, and positive.

The professional breakup causes an unnaturally high response rate. Once you add this to your sales tool kit, you will see it start to trigger activity. Scarcity increases desire.

Our objective through demand generation is to trigger attention and awareness for what we do and to get a buyer with a medium-to-high degree of influence on purchasing decisions to agree to a next step. That's it!

Introducing a structured and systematic approach will enable you to measure what's working and, more importantly, what's not. Are prospects engaging more with emails in week one or two? Which point of interest is getting a return call from a prospect? Over time, you can start to answer those questions and optimize your process based on the results.

 Pro Tip: SW³: Some will. Some won't. So what? Move on.

Some prospects will not be interested, which is fine. Some prospects will need what you do, which is excellent. Finally, some prospects will be on the fence, perhaps because they did not understand there was an opportunity to achieve a better business outcome from your product or service. This is where great salespeople differentiate themselves from others. They engage the "maybes" and convert them into "yeses."

What Exactly Do You Do in the First Conversation?

POWERFUL PROSPECTING PROCESS/CONVERSATION

INTRO AND RAPPORT	IDENTIFY NEEDS	DEVELOP NEEDS	VALUE PROPOSITION	CLOSE FOR NEXT STEPS
• Research – Person – Company – Point of Interest • Value Proposition (short) • Dimensions of Value	• Client wants / needs / opportunities (**3 Keys**) are foundation for a qualified sales cycle 1. _____ 2. _____ 3. _____	• How big a priority is addressing **3 Keys**? • What are the implications to the business if you do not address them?	• More detailed Value Proposition tied to their **3 Keys**	• Determine specifically where we go from here. • **Who** • **What** • **When**

GREAT QUESTIONS ALLOW YOU TO PROGRESS FROM STEP TO STEP

? **Why? / What? / How?**
Can you *tell me more*?

Of course, your initial conversation can go in many different directions, and preparing for every potential scenario is impossible. However, if you leverage our call process above, it will provide a helpful structure or guide for the call.

First, don't *pitch*—talk with them, not at them. A tactical salesperson in the 1990s used to be very good at pitching but didn't take the time to learn if their prospect even needed what they were selling. Today, you must solve a prospect's problem, and the starting point is to have them communicate the problem.

Leverage your clear and concise value proposition and point of interest so they can determine why they should listen to you and why they should care.

Preparation is critical. Drop your point of interest early in the conversation (in the first ten to fifteen seconds). This will show the prospect that you're not just dialing names from a list like lousy salespeople did forty years ago. You have researched and at least understand *something* about them and their business. Talk about them to stand out as a professional salesperson and differentiate yourself from three-quarters of the other salespeople. Everything is about them. As soon as you bring up these points, they'll realize you're unique, different, and better than most salespeople they receive calls from every day. This is your best chance of earning the right to a few minutes of their time.

Identify Needs
Once you break through "the wall" and engage in an authentic conversation, the next step is getting (and keeping) them talking. You need to discover what's going on with them, their business, their goals and objectives.

This is where your questions' quality determines the call's quality. It is best to have good open-ended questions that probe deeper into the problems they may be having or the objectives they are trying to achieve. Always preface a question with who, what, when, why, where, or how in order to get them to speak more. Start with a suitable surface-level question and dig deeper. Here's an example: "How do you compete and win in the market?"

As you dig in with the prospect, there is no substitute for genuine curiosity. Ask questions you want to know the answers to, not just because they are next on your list. I promise that this will lead to deeper, higher-quality conversations.

Develop Needs

As you keep asking open-ended questions and your prospect gets more comfortable, you will get a general idea of what's working and what's not. You want to dig deeper by following up with more open-ended questions that help expose the root of their problems. Let them talk but keep guiding them during this stage. The best way to do that is to ask them more about an issue. **For example:**

> "Tell me more about why that hasn't been working."
> "Tell me more about what success in this area looks like for your company in a year."
> "Tell me more about how you compete and win in your markets."

Once those needs are precise for your prospect, you need them to tell you how big a priority it is to address them. **For example:**

> "How big a priority is addressing (x) this year?
> "What would happen if you didn't address (x) this year?"
> Add multipliers…*why? Tell me more.*

Remember that for many people, opening up about problems they are having is not exactly the easiest or most comfortable thing to do—especially to a salesperson whom they have known for eight minutes! I like to try to *give permission* for them to admit that they have problems by reinforcing that it's OK. **For example**, I might say something like:

"Ah, I have heard that from a few of our customers."
"Yes, that's something that we hear a lot these days."

I have found these phrases to be disarming and allow the prospect to share more with me.

More importantly, it's the truth. Many customers have the same issues or challenges:

1. **They cannot predictably grow their sales.**
2. **They aren't adding enough new sales opportunities to the top of their funnel.**
3. **They don't sell on value; they sell on price.**
4. **Their sales opportunities stall, or the prospect stops returning their calls.**
5. **They experience high churn with new sales hires.**

Value Proposition

Now that you understand your prospect's problem(s), you need to offer them value to continue the conversation with you. For most of us in professional sales, we are not trying to win a sale in one call; instead, we are trying to earn the right to continue to the next stage of the sales process. Take about thirty seconds to a minute to explain your value proposition, and once they clearly understand what you do, tie it to the problems they identified through your questions. **For example:** "It sounds like your problem (x) is something we might be able to help solve, and we have worked with many similar companies that have had this problem."

Tying their needs to your solution is something you can do only if you take the time to learn about them and engage them with great questions.

Remember: you aren't pitching; you are problem-solving or adding value and insight.

Close for Next Steps

The last step of the call comes back to the preparation you did when you outlined the best-case scenario for the call. Do you want to close them on the spot? (Likely not.) Do you want to schedule a follow-up call in a few days? Do you want to send them a demo (I hope not, because by now you should know that most demos don't work because they are pitches, not conversations)? This will all depend on how your sales process is structured.

When you've proposed your solution, your follow-up should be something like, "Is any of this resonating with you?" or "Where would you like to go from here?" If you built the need correctly and tied it to a problem they have, chances are they will be interested. You can also be a bit more direct and specific; for example, if your firm sold financial reporting software, the end of the conversation might go something like this:

> *"Diane, it sounds like your operations team spends multiple days at the end of each month trying to reconcile disparate accounting systems manually. Your team has the exact problem that our software solution was intentionally created to solve. Would you be open to spending twenty minutes speaking to Gerry Smythe on our team about this? Gerry is an expert in this field and has worked with dozens of firms like yours. He will be able to showcase whether there may be an opportunity for Super Corp to improve in this area."*

Exercise: Leverage the power of the peloton for demand generation.
The peloton is the leading group or pack of riders in a road bicycle race. Riders in a group save energy by riding close (drafting or slipstreaming) behind other riders. The reduction in drag is dramatic; riding in the middle, the drag can be reduced to as little as 5–10 percent.

As salespeople, we need to be able to create demand for our businesses. We need to be able to fill the top of the "sales funnel" with sales opportunities from new logos or current customers.

However, demand generation is also the main activity that most salespeople avoid, and it is the number one reason they don't hit their goals and objectives.

Here's a way to leverage the power of the peloton to elevate the way you do demand generation. You can lead this as a sales leader or organize this as a member of the sales team.

Schedule a "call blitz" with the entire sales team one or two weeks out.

You kick off the call blitz with the whole team at 8:00 a.m., have each person quickly review the twenty calls that they are going to make during the blitz, and at 8:20, they start reaching out.

At 11:00 a.m., you regroup with the entire team and have each person summarize:

- how many dials they made (exactly)
- how many live (quality) conversations they had
- how many appointments they booked

When you regroup, you will find that a few team members have had some success. Success is progress, not perfection; in this case, it might mean that they had some quality conversations that went well (now they know they can do it), or they may have even booked a meeting or two.

Sometimes, you need to get the entire sales team in a position where they have no option but to make the calls. The "power of the peloton" defined above comes into play.

Every Saturday morning in the spring and summer I leverage the power of the peloton. I have a group of cyclists that I ride thirty to forty miles with (it's super fun). However, there are the odd Saturdays that I might prefer to stay in my cozy bed at 5:45. The fact that I have teammates waiting for me to ride gives me the motivation to get up and get going.

Fifteen minutes into each ride, I am glad I did get out of bed.

As a sales manager, one of the most motivating things you can do during these call blitzes is make calls with the team. Get on the phone and do it yourself. They love seeing you rolling up the sleeves and doing the work. This shows the team that you are not asking them to do anything you wouldn't do yourself.

Our demand generation program aims to start a sales cycle with a buyer with a medium-to-high degree of influence over purchasing our product or service. Once we successfully start this process, we must understand how to progress it. In short, we need to understand the separate and distinct steps to complete a sale for our business. That's the topic of the next chapter.

It's important to note that the topic of demand generation is one of the most widely researched and taught in professional sales because it's so difficult to do well and so dynamic. Anything that works tends to be replicated and saturated in the market through marketing automation technology, so you need to A/B test and adjust constantly.

Justin Michael is one of the best thought leaders in the demand generation prospecting space. His amazing book *Sales Superpowers* takes research and insight on demand generation to the next level and curates some of the best thinking in this area to help you "Turn outbound from a struggle to a craft and an art form. You start investing in others, learning from them, and enjoying that exchange of ideas. Prospecting becomes learning and growing versus hustling, grinding, and slogging."[15]

CHAPTER SUMMARY

- Opening is the new closing in professional B2B sales.
- All salespeople need to prioritize consistent demand generation, regardless of how amazing their products and services are.
- Demand generation is the X factor of professional sales because 80 percent of salespeople try to avoid doing it.
- Make first contact leveraging a consistent, systematic, multichannel sequence.
    - It takes at least seven to twelve reach-outs to connect with a buyer today.
- Leverage five great questions to drive the conversation.
- In your first conversation:
    - Build rapport.
    - Identify a need.
    - Develop the need.
    - Close for next steps.
- Make the conversation about *them*, not *you*.
- You have two ears and one mouth; use them in that proportion on a sales call.
- Be authentically curious.

Chapter 5

SALES PROCESS, STRATEGY, AND THE BUYER'S JOURNEY

"You won't believe it, Mark; we just closed our two quickest deals ever, even though we added more steps to the sales process, as you suggested!"

"Well, Dave...I'm thrilled to hear that."

I was catching up with one of my training customers to get an update on the progress they had recently made.

Risk Control Technologies, Inc. (RCT) was a fast-growing technology company specializing in risk management software for the insurance industry—a target market of customers known more for their notoriously slow pace of change than for their appetite for taking risks on new projects. Founded by two great young guys, both named Dave (Da Costa and Hanley), the company was doing well, but we all believed they could do better.

When I first met the Daves, I compared them to the most talented hockey players from Canada's tiniest, most northern town. They got by on their natural energy, enthusiasm, and talent, but they needed access to some best practices to hone their skills and take them to the major leagues. With some training and coaching, I could help these amazing entrepreneurs up their sales game to the highest levels.

One of the first things we did was discuss some ongoing opportunities that were in their pipeline. I immediately noticed that several deals were stalled in the final stages due to the prospect springing a last-minute IT review on them. In the best-case scenario, this review would occur, and the deal would get back on track and close. In the worst case, the IT group would get upset if they felt the business team was going around them and try to kill the deal, throwing Dave and Dave into a tailspin. Generally, they could get it back on the rails, but this dynamic had caused undue stress and jeopardized several sales in recent months.

After reviewing a few of these problem deals, I asked, "What if *we* proposed an IT review early in the sales process to ensure this doesn't happen?"

"Well, I guess we are always afraid that the IT team might push back, and the deal might not progress. We always hope the business team can drive the deal from start to finish."

I thought briefly and then asked, "Have you ever closed a deal *without* an IT review?"

The Daves looked across the table at each other, thought for a few seconds, then said almost in unison, "Nope."

That was all I needed to hear.

The Daves and I mapped out a sales process (which included an IT review stage) that hugely impacted their business in the next eighteen months. Sales more than doubled, and the velocity of their deals increased despite expanding their process to include more activities.

Of course, there were other things that we worked on, but aligning their sales process to the prospect's buying journey was critical. This also helped disqualify wrong-fit prospects earlier in the sales process. Dave and Dave were well on their way to the big leagues!

This chapter is about what happens once your demand-generation activities have created a qualified sales opportunity for your business. At this point, you must execute a sales process that identifies you as the better provider for your prospect to do business with while working with the customer to understand the impact your solution can have on their business and the financial model that cost-justifies it. Your process must support and align with your buyer's purchasing journey.

In the context of Dave and Dave's dilemma, they knew no company would purchase their product without having the IT team review it, but they were hesitant to add more steps to an already slow process. Little did they know that *adding* steps would increase the speed of their sales cycle!

The Sales Process

What do you have to do to sell better? As we noted in our discussion about your value proposition, professional sales is about solving a problem for a prospect or helping them capitalize on an opportunity. To effectively do that, you need to understand three things:

1. **Your Sales Process.** What steps or stages do you need to go through from an initial conversation to getting a deal done?
2. **Your Sales Strategy.** What methodology will earn you the right to successfully progress along each step of the sales process and win?

3. **Your Buyer's Journey.** What is the buyer going through on their side of this decision to investigate, explore, assess, and decide on the options available to solve a particular business problem or take advantage of a potential business opportunity?

Most salespeople either lack a well-defined process or don't follow the process that has been prescribed for them by their companies. They pitch and hope someone will buy their product or service simply because they made it available. They rely on the prospect to determine why they should buy the product and how to justify the investment cost.

When formulating a sales process, it helps to think of separate and distinct steps that are repeatable, manageable, and trainable. Without understanding these steps as a process to start and close a sale for your business, sales pursuits become a series of unrelated events that are very difficult to understand, track progress, or improve upon.

The sales process (like any process) is intended to capture a methodology of experience, wisdom, and best practices. When you map out these best practices as a process, it will enable you to:

- measure progress
- understand if, when, or why your process stalls
- strategize on how to move forward successfully

Understanding your sales activities as a process also simplifies your objectives and desired outcomes from critical meetings and interactions with buyers. Your sales process becomes a checklist of what you need to do to progress a sales opportunity from start to finish.

One of the core principles of any process is that you must complete each stage to move to the next stage. You must also understand that skipping steps lowers your likelihood of winning the deal.

One of the best analogies to underscore the importance of a set sales process is to compare it to dating. In my late twenties, I had the unbelievable luck of meeting a beautiful young lady in the lineup at a popular bar in Toronto. It was a freezing evening, but somehow, I convinced this girl to go out on a date with me, even though my two friends and I probably looked immature and ridiculous drinking cold beers in the lineup at a bar on the coldest night of the year in Toronto (and that's saying something).

One date led to the next, and by about the fourth dinner, I had this epiphany that this gorgeous girl was intelligent, funny, kind, and fun to be around. I thought she could be the one! The truth was, she was way out of my league, and if I had suggested that we become exclusive or move in together then and there, I can say with certainty that she would have politely excused herself to go to the restroom and then run out of the restaurant (and my life).

I couldn't "close the sale" without going through each stage success-fully. The better strategy (and thankfully the one I employed) was to be good enough on each date to earn the right for the next one and the next one. This occurred 328 times (maybe an exaggeration) before we moved in together, and she finally agreed to marry me. I dedicate this book to that amazing soulmate—my lovely wife, Donna.

You get it...skipping steps does *not* get you to a sale faster! It lowers your chances of success.

A straightforward sales process can be broken down into these stages:

1. Create Demand
2. Approach
3. Discover
4. Propose
5. Close

THE ITF SALES PROCESS

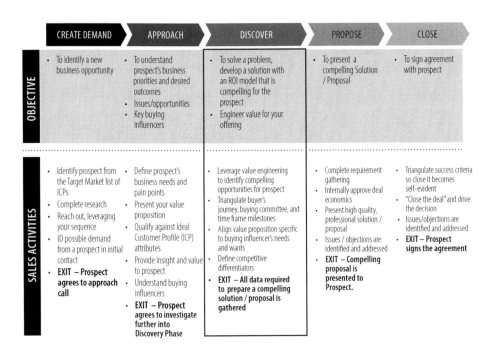

	CREATE DEMAND	APPROACH	DISCOVER	PROPOSE	CLOSE
OBJECTIVE	• To identify a new business opportunity	• To understand prospect's business priorities and desired outcomes • Issues/opportunities • Key buying influencers	• To solve a problem, develop a solution with an ROI model that is compelling for the prospect • Engineer value for your offering	• To present a compelling Solution / Proposal	• To sign agreement with prospect
SALES ACTIVITIES	• Identify prospect from the Target Market list of ICPs • Complete research • Reach out, leveraging your sequence • ID possible demand from a prospect in initial contact • **EXIT – Prospect agrees to approach call**	• Define prospect's business needs and pain points • Present your value proposition • Qualify against Ideal Customer Profile (ICP) attributes • Provide insight and value to prospect • Understand buying influencers • **EXIT – Prospect agrees to investigate further into Discovery Phase**	• Leverage value engineering to identify compelling opportunities for prospect • Triangulate buyer's journey, buying committee, and time frame milestones • Align value proposition specific to buying influencer's needs and wants • Define competitive differentiators • **EXIT – All data required to prepare a compelling solution / proposal is gathered**	• Complete requirement gathering • Internally approve deal economics • Present high quality, professional solution / proposal • Issues / objections are identified and addressed • **EXIT – Compelling proposal is presented to Prospect.**	• Triangulate success criteria so close it becomes self-evident • "Close the deal" and drive the decision • Issues/objections are identified and addressed • **EXIT – Prospect signs the agreement**

Your main intention in every interaction at every stage must *always* be to help your prospect make the right purchasing decision with insight, guidance, and value. If you prioritize making a sale over providing value and sincerely helping your prospects, you will have a short career in professional sales.

You can download the IN THE FUNNEL Solution Sales Process here:

https://www.inthefunnel.com/ltls-sales-tools

Password: thesellingwell

Let's review each stage of the sales process in detail.

Step 1. Create Demand

Your objective is to add new potential business opportunities into your sales pipeline constantly. We call this "filling the top of the funnel." Entrepreneurs and salespeople alike must always fill the top of the funnel with new sales opportunities to succeed.

This is where we engage prospects from our ICP list to initiate attention, interest, and action. We want to connect with buyers, share our value proposition, learn about them, and drive interest in a second meeting to continue the conversation.

Pro Tip: Always focus on providing insight and value in every conversation with a customer or prospect.

During this stage, we want to get the answers to two fundamental qualification questions:

1. **Are we talking to the right company?**
   a. Do they meet some of the essential criteria of our ICP (size, scale, location, industry, compelling business problem)?

2. **Are we talking to the right person (buyer)?**
   a. Do they have a medium-to-high degree of influence over a decision to purchase our solution?

If we can answer yes to these questions, it is worth our time (and theirs) to proceed to the next step. We know we have completed this stage when the buyer agrees to a second meeting with us.

Step 2. Approach

This is a prescheduled meeting with the right buyer at the right company. In this meeting, we want to briefly remind them of our value proposition and, more importantly, learn about *them*.

You want to learn about their business goals and objectives and how they are progressing. You want to know what they are trying to achieve and why. You also want to understand this buyer's needs and wants. What is important to them and why?

In truth, they want to talk about themselves. Harvard researchers Diana Tamir and Jason Mitchell have documented that people get a neurochemical buzz from telling stories and self-disclosure.[16] I'm sure you have experienced this at a cocktail party or networking event—you engage with someone you feel is a great conversationalist, only to leave the interaction realizing that you barely asked them anything about themselves. You got to talk about yourself to someone who seemed genuinely interested, and it felt great.

Your buyers may resist sharing information with you. Your job is to earn the right to break through that resistance by providing value and offering insight. This happens naturally when you showcase high levels of:

- curiosity
- business acumen
- industry acumen
- empathy

The approach stage of the sales process aims to earn the right to move into a deeper discovery with the prospect. Here's an example of how we might move from the approach phase into the discovery phase.

Alison (Buyer): *"Mark, your sales training program looks interesting, but we've invested lots of money in sales training in the past with well-known large sales training companies and have little to show for it. Based on what you have heard, can you help us get a different result?"*

Me (Seller): *"Well, Alison, I'm not sure now. Your firm certainly has some challenges we have solved with companies like PureFacts and Strategic Coach, but every environment is unique and different. We can do a one- to two-hour deeper dive with you to determine whether or not we can help with your sales strategy, structure, team, processes, technology, and tools. As part of this process, I also like to interview a few of your salespeople briefly to get their perspectives on what type of help they could use.*

Once we better understand these things and map out specific desired business outcomes from sales training, we can collectively decide if there is an ROI here that makes sense for your company.

By the way, if we determine that we are not a good fit to help you achieve those desired business outcomes, I'll let you know that, too. Either way, once we understand your environment a little better, I will recommend how to elevate sales performance whether you engage with us or not, so this will be worth your time. Shall we book the discovery session?"

Alison (Buyer): *"Let's do it."*

Step 3. Discover

One of the most common questions that I'm asked during our sales training workshops is, "How do I close better?" Everyone is looking for the silver bullet trick or tactic to help them magically close deals. Sorry, but this is the most significant lie from the unrealistic stereotypes of professional salespeople: that you can drag or coax someone into a sale by sweet-talking and "closing" them.

My advice: If you want to win more sales, get better at discovery.

Discovery is the most critical stage of our sales process because you learn more about the prospect and their desired business outcomes. The more you understand their business, goals, objectives, and current challenges, the better your chances of figuring out how to help.

Top salespeople enjoy discovery. Some people literally get a buzz from being authentically curious and learning about others, as Diane Hamilton explains in *Cracking the Curiosity Code*: "Pursuing whatever makes us curious triggers that gene, and dopamine is released into our bodies when curiosity is triggered. Dopamine is sometimes called the 'reward molecule' because it makes us feel good."[17]

Andy Paul, one of the top minds in professional sales, says: "Your job as a seller is to listen to understand what the most important thing is to your buyer. And then help them get it."[18]

A great discovery is driven by solid and prepared questions that enable you to understand better your prospect's desired business outcomes and what, if anything, is preventing them from achieving them.

Great questions drive discovery, but frequently the first answer is just the start of the conversation. Often, the second or third add-on question uncovers the real opportunities. For example, when we are selling sales training, we often ask about the growth goals for the business. **Here's an example:**

> *Mark (Seller): "Alison, what are the company's growth objectives this year?"*
>
> *Alison (Buyer): "This year, and every year, we need to grow by a minimum of 30 percent."*
>
> *Mark (Seller): Add on the question, "Why?"*
>
> *Alison (Buyer): "Because the value of our software company increases dramatically if we can show 30 percent year-over-year growth consistently."*
>
> *Mark (Seller): "I got it and thank you." Add on the question, "How are you doing against that goal?"*
>
> *Alison (Buyer): "Not so good. Half the year is over, and we are trending toward about 11 percent year-over-year growth."*

> **Mark (Seller):** *"Ouch. What are the implications to the business if we don't halt that trend?"*
>
> **Alison (Buyer):** *"Very significant. If we need to re-forecast, we will need to downsize, and the board will be none too happy with the sales team and me."*
>
> **Mark (Seller):** *"Yikes! What are the top reasons that sales are down, in your view?"*
>
> **Alison (Buyer):** *"How long do you have for this meeting?"*

Of course, this conversation will likely continue for another thirty minutes, with every question intended to help us better understand what's preventing them from hitting their goals.

Please note that at this point we have not talked about how great the ITF sales training is, we are not pitching at them, we are discovering what their issues and opportunities are.

 Download our best-questions formula here:
https://www.inthefunnel.com/ltls-sales-tools
Password: thesellingwell

During discovery, remember the age-old proverb in sales, "People don't buy drill bits; they buy a way to hang a picture on the wall." You aren't in front of the prospect to tell them how strong or sharp your drill bit is...you are there to figure out how they can make their living room more beautiful.

The discovery stage allows you to roll up your sleeves with the prospect and collaboratively determine whether your solution will add value. We exit the discovery phase when we clearly understand the compelling reason to move forward with your solution and financial business case that justifies the investment for the customer.

 Pro Tip: If there is no compelling reason for the prospect to buy your solution, either keep working through the discovery stage or disengage. Don't try to sell anyone something they don't need. Sell without selling out (and a tip of the cap again to Andy Paul).

Step 4. Propose

This is the stage that most salespeople prematurely jump to.

Remember my story about meeting my wife, Donna? I couldn't wait to ask her to move in with me...but if I had asked too soon, I would have had little to no chance of winning that "sale." We didn't know each other well enough for that kind of commitment.

The same is true in our professional sales process. Don't bother proposing or pricing anything formally unless you already know what the return on investment is for the prospect. Also, remember that *your* opinion on the return on investment only matters if the prospect has built the model alongside you or, at a minimum, has validated it.

Your prospects need help answering these questions:

- Why should they buy from you?
- Why should they buy from you *now*?

If you cannot objectively answer these questions because you need more information, then stay in the discovery stage of your sales process until you have the answers. If you can't answer these questions because you cannot objectively add any value to this prospect, then politely disengage. Don't waste time selling to people who are never going to buy.

Another critical element of this stage of the sales process is to understand precisely what happens with our proposal once we give it to them. Specifically:

- **Who decides on this proposal?**
- **What is most important to each person regarding our solution and why?**
- **How/when will they make the decision?**
- **Who needs to approve the spending further?**
- **What are the implications of not moving ahead with this proposal?**
- **Who believes this is the right thing to do, and who doesn't? We need to know why in each case.**

How do we find out the answers to these questions? That's easy...we ask! Believe it or not, prospects are generally open to sharing this information with you. After all, if they like and trust you and believe your solution can help their business, they have a vested interest in understanding this to better navigate their processes internally.

Don't throw that proposal over the fence without walking the prospect through it in a live conversation.

I firmly believe that no proposal should ever be "thrown over the fence" (or, more accurately, today, emailed to the prospect without a discussion). I recommend that when presenting a proposal—and notice I used the term *presenting*—this should be done live with the customer in person or over a video conference. This allows you to ask validating questions and receive verbal and nonverbal feedback. It also gives you one last chance to make minor modifications before sending it to the prospect. The proposal presentation is a valuable interaction opportunity that should not be skipped.

Pro Tip: Your proposal or solution may "travel" within your prospect's organization without you. When you finally email it to them, provide a five-bullet summary of the key points so that an executive receiving it can review the summary. I love to capture this summary in a short video that our buyers can share within their organization.

Step 5. Close

We move to the closing stage only once we have received a verbal commitment from the prospect. A verbal commitment is someone with authority telling us that we have won and that they want to move forward.

In the closing stage, we focus on the activities required to negotiate agreements (including final pricing) and sign the contract. This is a critical point worth emphasizing: *don't negotiate the price until you know you have won.*

Too often, we get lured into dropping prices before winning a deal, which helps the prospect negotiate with their preferred provider. We need to ask for the business if and only if we have earned the right to do so by providing a compelling business case for the customer to proceed with us.

 Pro Tip: If someone asks for a discount, respond with, "I'm not sure I can provide a 5 percent discount and will have to work with the finance team internally. But if we can do that, are we saying we have a deal? Also, my finance team is going to ask me two questions before they respond:

- How did you come up with the target of a 5 percent reduction?
- Are you negotiating with us exclusively or with multiple vendors?"

They ask this because they will not provide any movement unless we have won and are in exclusive negotiations.

The Buyer's Journey

Now, let's consider the other (more critical side) of the same coin. The buyer's journey comprises all the activities that occur in parallel to your sales process. You may view yourself as the conductor moving the wand to your sales process, but the prospect's band needs to hit the notes.

Several models out there map the stages of the buyer's journey, including one from the Gartner Group that is commonly referred to as the "spaghetti diagram" due to the myriad of twists and turns the buyer's journey often takes. One of our favorite perspectives on the buyer's journey comes from Frank Cespedes, a senior lecturer at Harvard

Business School and author of *Sales Management That Works: How to Sell in a World That Never Stops Changing.*[19]

Cespedes advises that buyers work through the following parallel activities when making a purchasing decision:

- explore
- evaluate
- engage
- experience

These activities are not serial or linear. The buyer starts, stops, progresses, and even reverses along this process before making a final decision.

As you progress along your sales process, you need to think about your buyer's view of what is happening. You might be thinking, "Come on, Mark...you're telling me I not only have to follow my *own* sales process, but I also have to help my prospect navigate *their* internal process?" Yes, you do. Let me rephrase this answer...if you want to be an effective salesperson who constantly outperforms the competition, then yes, you do!

One of the biggest challenges for sellers is understanding where the buyer is in their journey at any point in time and providing value, insight, support, and guidance to help them build consensus for the right decision. This does not always mean that their journey will end up with them purchasing from you; instead, it should result in making the best decision for them and their business.

In today's information-rich world, the buyer has often progressed along their purchasing journey a long way before engaging with you as a seller. In 2017, CEB, now owned by Gartner, found that buyers are on average 57 percent of the way through their process before reaching out to your firm based on online information, referrals, or marketing information they may have obtained.[20]

Given this fact, we need to ensure that when we connect with a prospect for a live conversation, we provide maximum value by making the conversation about them. Don't simply regurgitate features to the buyer that they have probably already read about online. You need to understand what *desired outcome* is driving their need for a product or service, and to do that, you need to earn the right to get them to open up and have an authentic conversation with you.

On initial contact with new buyers, you can accomplish this by:

- **Completing research on every lead before engaging (this is a far quicker process than most think). Before picking up the phone, take a few minutes to do your research. It will show.**
- **Planning for every follow-up meeting with your buyers to ensure you add real value for them in every interaction.**
- **Understanding that every interaction with a buyer is an opportunity to stand out over your competition. Treat these events as the *final interview* for a job you want!**

The buyer begins to understand that you, as a seller, have their best interests as your priority. This customer-centric approach to selling is one of the best and easiest ways to differentiate your company from your competitors. How well you sell will set you apart when products and services become increasingly commoditized.

You might wonder, "How do we differentiate with service if the prospect has not purchased yet?" The answer lies in how well you sell. Your knowledge, guidance, expertise, responsiveness, and overall ease of doing business will be how you become the company that wins deals because you *sold better*. Buyers select the sellers who know them and their businesses better than the competition.

The IN THE FUNNEL Strategy Builder

The sales process outlines the steps to start and complete a sale from the seller's perspective.

Your sales strategy is the approach you take to ensure that you successfully progress through each step of your sales process.

As you navigate a sales process, constantly ask yourself two critical questions:

- **What are my chances of winning this deal?**
- **How do I improve my chances of winning this deal?**

A strong salesperson will constantly assess each deal objectively to improve their chances (or probability) of winning.

At the core of the sales strategy is the ability to navigate the various buyers who influence a corporate purchasing decision and then be able to address the following:

- **their professional needs and wants**
- **their emotional needs and wants**
- **their degree of influence on the purchasing decision**
- **how they feel about your solution**

The research consistently says that corporate decisions today continue to be made by committees. On average, somewhere between six and eight people are involved in B2B purchasing decisions of any considerable size.[21] So, to win a deal, we need to understand who those six to eight buyers are and address their personal and professional wants and needs relating to the agreement. This is the essence of sales strategy.

Another critical piece of knowledge we, as sellers, need to be armed with is understanding the competitive environment in which we play. Suppose we don't know the other solutions the prospect may look at. How will we clarify to the buyers why we think we are a better option to help them achieve their desired business outcomes and personal wins?

 Here's a short video and tool to help you build a sales strategy for a vital sale. This is the ITF Strategy Builder: https://www.inthefunnel.com/ltls-sales-tools *Password: thesellingwell*

To effectively leverage the ITF Strategy Builder in your organization, we recommend taking a point-in-time snapshot of how you are doing on any important deal (and let's be honest, which ones aren't important?). Next, you can workshop ideas with your team on how to improve your strategic positioning. This is one area of professional sales where team collaboration is precious.

If you have a simple and consistent framework for assessing your strategic positioning on an opportunity, then you can:

- **share the status of the deal with your teammates**
- **collaborate with the team on how to improve your situation (and your probability of winning)**

Strategy is one of the most overlooked elements of professional sales because most of us get so caught up in creating the solution for the deal and then writing the proposal (or filling out the two-inch-thick

RFP) that we neglect the most critical question: *Do we have a logical strategy to win this deal?*

For our must-win deals in a given quarter, the critical question we must ask ourselves is, "What do I do next?" Too often, salespeople sit back and *hope* they win the deal.

While discussing sales strategy, we must tip our hat to Robert B. Miller and Stephen E. Heiman, who wrote the seminal work in this area in 1985, *The New Strategic Selling*. I see traces of their work in dozens of great sales books. Clearly, our model has been influenced by their amazing thinking almost forty years back.

 Pro Tip: *Hope* is not a sales strategy!

There is one last (critical) point to note before moving to the next chapter. Even if we think we are in a leading, "can't possibly lose" position on a deal, we still want to assess our situation. Just as the football team leading the game 27–7 in the third quarter still comes out and plays hard in the fourth, we sellers cannot rest on our laurels when we feel the deal is in the bag. As both Yogi Berra and Lenny Kravitz will tell you, "It ain't over 'til it's over."

CHAPTER SUMMARY

- Selling well means understanding the interplay between your sales process, the buyer's journey, and your overall sales strategy.
- A sales process refers to the separate and distinct steps to completing a sale for your business, from initial conversation to getting a deal done. They are:
    a. Create Demand
    b. Approach
    c. Discover
    d. Propose
    e. Close
- A sales strategy is your game plan to address the needs and wants of buyers who influence the purchasing decision.
- If you skip steps in your sales process, you diminish your chances of winning the sale.
- You earn the right to help a prospect by adding value and insight into each and every conversation with them.

Chapter 6

THE SALES TECH STACK

When I played goalie in competitive ice hockey over thirty years ago, almost every save I made was painful. The equipment available to protect goalies was woefully inadequate, and my gear was not top-of-the-line. I had a good mask and excellent goalie gloves, but everything else was subpar.

Frighteningly, my throat and chest area were not well protected, so every time a player took a slap shot at me, my first thought was, "Do not let this puck hit you in the throat." My secondary priority was ensuring that the puck didn't get into the net. Because my equipment was so inadequate, I couldn't focus on my primary objective.

We played tons of games and had even more practice in my five years playing at that level. Due to some bad luck and the law of averages, I broke multiple fingers, was concussed more than once, and had the very "enlightening" experience of trying to breathe after taking a puck to the throat.

By the end of that career, I was *so happy* to relinquish my goalie pads. I no longer had to worry about the pain.

About fifteen years ago, I decided to join a men's recreational league (or "beer league" as we call it as adults) to try to get back in the net. Once I got back on the ice, I had a revelation. The new equipment technology was vastly more protective than anything I had ever used. I'm not talking about marginal improvement...the difference was night and day. Now, a puck to the chest from point-blank...no problem. There was little chance of getting through the protection due to the new and excellent throat guards attached to every goalie helmet.

What was most amazing to me was that when I was in the heat of the game, I had one single priority: saving the puck from going into the net. When I no longer had to worry about getting injured, I could focus 100 percent on reading the plays and reacting quickly to make every save. I reignited my passion and energy for this sport I loved in my youth.

- **Technology has completely changed how I play goalie in hockey.**
- **Technology changes everything and will transform your future if you embrace it.**
- **Technology has absolutely changed modern professional selling, but not in every aspect.**

The importance of connection and authentic curiosity for the buyer and their business has not changed in one-hundred-plus years of professional selling. Nor will it change in the next thirty. We will always need to be able to engage in an authentic conversation with our prospects about how we can improve their future to earn the right to work with them.

What has changed, however, is *how* we initiate those conversations. This is particularly true for the top-of-funnel activities. In other words, those activities that enable us to have:

*The right **conversation** with the right **person** at the right **time**.*

One of the best resources I have found on sales tech is *Tech-Powered Sales* by Justin Michael and Tony Hughes. I love their book because it combines modern sales techniques and technologies with fundamental truths about core selling principles. Justin and Tony tell us that over five thousand technologies are focused on enabling salespeople to succeed, and billions of venture capital dollars have flooded into this lucrative market in the last several years alone.[22]

Collectively, the set of technology tools you use in your day-to-day sales efforts is called the "sales tech stack."

This chapter is your simple guide to the world of the sales tech stack. We'll begin by highlighting some high-level categories for the simple sales tech stack and a few examples of key technology providers in those categories today. Note: technologies change daily, so depending on when you read this book, classes and essential providers of the tech stack may change dramatically.

 Check out an interview with Justin and Tony on my podcast, The *Selling Well*.
https://www.inthefunnel.com/podcast

 Pro Tip: With the sales tech stack (as with anything), complexity is the enemy of execution. We all must focus on simplifying how we leverage these to maximize the return on investment.

Technology will never absolve our salespeople of the need to initiate an engaging conversation with a prospective customer and provide insight and value. Having the right conversation is the core job of everyone in professional sales. However, in some cases, technology can help us find the right *person* to speak with and alert us at the right *time* to have that conversation.

As you explore the various solutions you may want to include in your sales tech stack, one of the things I have found very useful is tapping into the many great YouTube videos that provide training and coaching on using virtually every single sales technology. For example, by searching YouTube for "LinkedIn Sales Navigator Tutorial," you will find hundreds of great videos that will help you determine whether this tool can be a valuable addition to the sales tech stack for your team.

These tutorials are often hosted by folks from outside the vendor company, external sales coaches, or salespeople interested in sharing their knowledge. These tutorials are a fantastic way of learning new technologies because you can learn at your own pace and rewind and rewatch at any time. If you dedicate even thirty minutes a week to this exercise, you will be amazed at how much you can learn about the latest sales tech tools over a year.

As my friend Dan Sullivan of Strategic Coach says, "Progress, not perfection." This is a great mantra when learning anything new, including new technologies. Let's explore several of the sales technology categories that any sales organization should consider for use in their operation.

Customer Relationship Management (CRM)

The sales tech stack started with Customer Relationship Management (CRM) software. Although there were several predecessors, the five-hundred-pound gorilla in this category is Salesforce. Salesforce kicked off a technology revolution in 1999 as one of the first companies (in any industry) to pioneer a cloud infrastructure along with browser-based user interfaces. At the core, CRM systems help sales organizations manage companies, contacts, activities, and specific sales opportunities in a centralized software database. The CRM often plugs into other elements of the sales tech stack to extend and enhance various features, functions, and data for the salespeople who use it daily.

Data Enrichment

The main goal of data enrichment platforms is to supplement user-entered data to provide salespeople with the most up-to-date information about prospects and customers. Since the business world is constantly in flux, with companies being acquired and people changing jobs, data enrichment platforms help fill in the blanks from a data perspective. Yes, George Clooney may have been a vice president for Strategic Coach when he was entered into our database, but in the past six months, he moved to become a senior consultant for IN THE FUNNEL. We may also have George's name and phone number, but the data enrichment platform can provide us with George's email address to supplement our outreach efforts. Without a data enrichment platform, our sales team would see out-of-date, incomplete information on George.

Intent Data

As scary as it may sound, most of us already know that we are being tracked and monitored in our everyday lives by many online sources. As a result, certain technology providers follow what people and companies are doing online and then package this information for sales as "intent data."

For example, suppose you sell CRM systems for a company like HubSpot and want to know which prospects are in the market for the solutions you provide at any given time. In this scenario, knowing which prospects in your target market have been doing online searches, reading blogs, and downloading white papers to obtain information on CRM systems would be beneficial. It would also be helpful to find out who has been searching for some of your main competitors (in our HubSpot example, who has been exploring Salesforce, Microsoft Dynamics, or Zoho).

This data tells you that these prospects may intend to investigate the offering you sell, so now would be an excellent time to reach out to them. Armed with this information, the demand-generation efforts focused on these target companies or individuals will have a higher success rate, given they have already expressed some intent to purchase a solution in your category.

Social Network Intelligence

What you can learn about somebody online today based on their digital footprint is amazing. The trail of data you leave behind you as you visit websites, interact with social media, send or open emails, download resources, or submit an online form is mind-boggling. Even the tone you use in posting blogs or commenting on a colleague's LinkedIn page can provide insights into your personality traits and tendencies.

In recent years, software solution providers have begun to leverage this digital footprint to complete a personality assessment on a potential buyer (leveraging IQ, EQ, and AI) to provide tips on how best to engage and communicate to ensure success in the sales process. For example, your approach to selling to someone with "impulsive" tendencies will be very different than when selling to someone flagged as "highly analytical." To make things even easier, many of these tools will draft emails and generate scripts that can be used during outreach or interactions with different personalities to help give salespeople a better chance of success.

Trigger Events

Change is a constant in business. People change jobs (on average once every three years), companies acquire other firms, or businesses make strategic decisions to enter or exit particular markets.

These changes always impact the status quo and provide potential opportunities for sellers trying to penetrate new accounts. Timing is everything, so reaching out to help your prospects during these events may increase your chances of connecting with them. They may be more open to advice, insight, and options amid change.

Imagine one of your best customers is the VP of human resources working for Citibank. When that VP leaves CitiBank and joins American Express, within about ninety days, she will likely assess the environment within American Express and develop her plan for any necessary changes. She will likely leverage the strategies, processes, tools, and partners she has used in her previous role, so as a seller, you want to know that this trigger event has occurred so you can connect with her at the right time, i.e., when she is making change.

For the same reason (people make changes when they are new to a role), you will want to reach out to whoever replaced her in her old job as VP of human resources at Citibank.

In a different scenario, perhaps a new CIO was hired at Allstate Insurance, one of your competitor's best accounts. When this happens, you also need to know because typically, when a new executive takes on a role, they will be looking to make changes, and this may be the event you need to get your foot in the door to knock out an entrenched competitor. Trigger events are also a great reason to connect (or reconnect, depending on the event) to discuss upcoming business challenges or objectives your organization may be well suited to help with.

Of course, change can introduce risk within our customer base because existing strong relationships may disappear when people or circumstances change within your customer's organization. On the flip side (as outlined in the Allstate Insurance example), change provides you with opportunities within your competitor's accounts because *their* existing solid relationships may disappear, providing us a chance to penetrate that account.

Just as trigger events can occur with changes related to people, they can also prepare us to act regarding changes at the company level. Suppose you sell IT services and see that a company in your target market has acquired another business. In this scenario, now is likely a great time to contact them regarding potential upcoming systems integration projects, as they will need to integrate the business systems of the new entity into the existing ones.

Sequencers

Everyone is busy, so it isn't easy to connect with them to have a conversation. They have too much to do in too little time, so getting their attention as someone they do not yet know is extraordinarily difficult. Thankfully, sales outreach can take many forms:

- face-to-face
- video conference
- phone call
- voicemail
- text
- email
- video email
- website (chatbot)
- LinkedIn
- other social media message

As salespeople, we need help scheduling and tracking our multi-channel activities to make a successful first contact with a new buyer. The technology that enables this multichannel reach-out is called a "sequencer." Sequencers are powerful because they allow salespeople to perform automated tasks that appear to be custom/one-off to the person on the receiving end.

Initially referred to as "marketing automation," a sequencer is a valuable part of the sales tech stack. These tools allow salespeople to customize an automated and scheduled series of outreach efforts for a prospect based on templates. Some sequencers also allow for optimization using A/B testing, which gives us insights into which templates or approaches work best based on the actions taken by the buyers. This is where the science of sales meets the art.

Engagement

Engagement technologies exist to help us have better live conversations with customers. Some of these tools are ubiquitous, like Zoom and Microsoft Teams, which are used to collaborate with buyers. Others are more advanced conversational intelligence technologies like Gong or Salesloft. These solutions analyze sales calls and provide valuable real-time insight to help improve sales performance. This may include suggesting questions, changes in tone, or recommending specific product offerings based on what is said during the interaction.

Of course, the list of potential solutions you can add to your sales tech stack is never-ending. To avoid getting overwhelmed by the myriad of options, I always recommend starting small by prioritizing what will benefit your business and building out from there. Far too often, I work with customers who have made significant investments in technology tools only to find that their sales teams aren't using them properly (or at all!).

Pro Tip: Always set some expectations around the return on investment you believe you can achieve for every dollar you spend on your tech stack.

This brings us to the end of Part 1: Create Your Sales Plan. We have learned that there are five things we need to think about to convert our core business capability into revenue for our business:

1. Value proposition
2. Territory planning
3. Demand generation
4. Sales process, strategy, and the buyer's journey
5. Sales tech stack

In Part 2, Build Your Sales Team, we will consider the team that executes your sales playbook.

CHAPTER SUMMARY

- Thousands of technologies will help salespeople engage in the right conversation with the right prospect at the right time. These are collectively known as the sales tech stack.
- Keep it simple at first, and think about starting with these categories:
    a. CRM—track companies, contacts, and sales opportunities.
    b. Data enrichment—find updated information on contacts.
    c. Intent data—understand which companies are investigating the services you offer.
    d. Social network intelligence—learn about the people you are selling to.
    e. Trigger events—understand when human capital migration or corporate restructuring makes it an ideal time to connect with a buyer.
    f. Engagement software—improve your performance when you have live conversations.
- Ensure you have a business case and a return on investment for every dollar spent on the sales tech stack.
- Everyone in professional sales should get used to training themselves on the sales technologies they use. It's easy; search training videos on YouTube.

Part 2

BUILD YOUR SALES TEAM

Chapter 7

THE ART AND SCIENCE OF INTERVIEWING SALESPEOPLE

My stomach churned as I sat in the small meeting room, waiting for Jeremy to arrive. It wouldn't be an enjoyable meeting for me, and even less pleasant for Jeremy. It had been three months since I hired him for my team's sales role, and I realized he wasn't cut out for the job. What made it worse is that I really liked Jeremy...he was a great guy with a young family, and now I had to tell him he would no longer be working for IN THE FUNNEL.

"This stinks," I thought. "If only I could have figured this out during the interview."

Most sales leaders have gone through this scenario dozens of times.

You get what seems to be a great candidate and have an excellent feeling about them—only to discover you were dead wrong. Maybe after working with them, you find out that they aren't coachable, they lack drive, they won't pick up the phone to sell, or they had no idea what was truly expected of them in the role. In some cases, they just aren't cut out for sales. And then you must let them go.

This chapter aims to help you never have these feelings again with a new sales hire. Now, I don't want to set your expectations too high—although I will give you an excellent framework for interviewing salespeople, it's not foolproof. You should expect that no matter how rock solid your hiring process is, you may still hire someone who doesn't work out. The problematic nature of human resources is only amplified by salespeople being among the most challenging people to hire. Why? By nature, salespeople *sell*; *many* are good at selling hiring managers on why they should hire them! Once you have a solid process for interviewing and hiring, you can rely less on your intuition.

The Never-Ending Challenge of Recruiting in Professional Sales

I have been in professional sales for thirty years, and I have never seen such an enormous gap between the demand for competent professional salespeople and the supply of suitable candidates.

Now, there are lots of salespeople out there, and more are coming. Frank Cespedes from Harvard University estimates that around 50 percent of US college graduates, regardless of their majors, will work in sales at some point in their careers.[23] The issue is that there aren't enough well-trained, professional, competent salespeople.

Let's look at the actual costs to your business of hiring and replacing salespeople.

Executive search fees: Executive search fees range from 15–20 percent of the candidate's first-year base salary. If you are performing these recruiting tasks in-house, there are costs to your team's time and often fees for posting open roles on hiring websites.

Interview time: It can take significant time from executives and multiple team members to perform several rounds of interviews with candidates. That time is expensive for the company.

New hire ramp-up time: If done well, the new hire's onboarding process takes between six and nine months. During that time, you are paying the new sales hire to learn before you get much payback in new sales revenue.

Lost revenue: When sales territories are vacant, there are significant groups of prospects and customers that you are not selling to and not generating revenue from. Customer relationships and loyalty can also be negatively impacted when salespeople change repeatedly.

Given the black-and-white nature of the performance metrics available in sales, some of the high churn (30 percent) in professional sales is expected. However, the majority of the churn in sales comes from hiring the wrong people for sales roles or lowering their chances of success with a poor onboarding program.

One of our terrific customers is Berenson, Inc., a distributor of decorative and functional hardware in the kitchen cabinet industry. They are an amazing entrepreneurial success story, with the business currently being run by Evan Smith, a third-generation leader. Berenson has a fantastic customer-first and team-first culture, so employees love working there. Multiple members of the sales team have tenures of fifteen-plus years. It's a special place.

It's also an extremely well-run business. Evan is an engineer by training, and he's both detail- and process-oriented. The company leverages a formal management framework and runs a very tight ship.

However, when they were looking to expand the sales organization, they had significant difficulties interviewing and hiring the right person in sales or sales leadership. When they engaged IN THE FUNNEL for some consulting help, they had multiple examples of new hires lasting fewer than six months over the last few years. One initial area of focus was helping them expand the sales team.

After Evan and I applied the ITF interviewing methodology below, Berenson was delighted to welcome on board a new sales leader who was the right fit to enable their spectacular five-year growth plan.

Start with a Clear Job Description, Including Measures of Success

Take some time to think about the attributes you are looking for in a new sales team member. That way, you know what you are trying to learn in the interview process. Define what success will look like for the person in the role after three, six, and nine months. The more details here, the better it is for the candidate and you.

At IN THE FUNNEL, we hire on intelligence, drive, humility, optimism, and passion. We create a clear job description before interviewing anyone, so we are completely aligned on expectations.

 For a copy of our template job description for an account executive (direct contributor sales role), visit: https://www.inthefunnel.com/ltls-sales-tools
Password: thesellingwell

The Interview Process

As a starting point, I like the idea of interacting with a potential new hire at least three times before making them a job offer. To support this, the IN THE FUNNEL interview framework has a three-step interview process that can be completed in less than three weeks.

When hiring salespeople, time does matter because your best candidates will be interviewing with multiple companies at the same time they are interviewing with you. Always go into a hiring process with a sense of urgency and an expectation that you will compete with other companies for this individual.

The gold standard regarding the interviewing process comes from Geoff Smart and Randy Street in their fantastic book *Who*.[24] Leveraging their great work, we use the following procedure for interviewing new sales hires:

- Prescreening video
- Interview #1—top-grading interview
- Interview #2—ninety-day onboarding plan

Prescreening Video

Once you have identified a candidate that looks good on paper, send them a short video with this format:

1. Give a short introduction to your company. Include an overview of your value proposition to the market and to employees.
2. Request that they send you back a video answering the following questions:
   - Why did you respond to the job posting?
   - What do you want to do with your career?
   - What are you really good at professionally?
   - What are your income expectations?

In your message to them, include a link to whichever video technology you use (there are many of them out there) and include the free trial download link so they can install it themselves (most tools have them).

The video message you receive back from the candidate is a fantastic screening tool that will help you decide whether you want to move them to the next phase of the process—a face-to-face interview.

The first question you might ask is, "What if they can't use video technology?" Well, I believe all sales professionals today should be capable of emailing a video message to a prospect. If they have not yet used this technology, the link you send them in your message will enable them to learn how. Yes, this takes effort, but should you invest a full hour of your time interviewing them if they aren't willing to exert that effort? Also, do you want to hire them if they can't learn a straightforward new technology?

As a caveat, if you are in a more traditional industry (manufacturing, for example) where the salespeople are less technologically savvy, consider revising Phase 1 of the process to include a live twenty-minute telephone call or video conference prescreening interview to cover the content outlined above.

 Pro Tip: In the early stages of the interview process, the question is not, "Would I hire this person?" It's too early to be convinced that the candidate fits the company perfectly. In the early stages of the process, the question to answer is, "Has this person earned the right to proceed to the next stage of the interview process?"

First Interview: The Top-Grading Interview

One of the critical mistakes I see in interviews is the interviewer doing most of the talking (which typically continues for the entire interview once they get rolling!). The objective is to learn about the candidate.

There are two parts to an effective face-to-face top-grading interview:

Part 1: They walk you through their career chronologically (75 percent of the interview)

Part 2: You educate them on your business—specifically the role, company, culture, customers, and problems you solve for them (25 percent of the interview)

In Part 1, for each significant job or role, ask them to address the following questions:

1. What were you hired to do?
2. What were your major accomplishments in that role?
3. What were the more challenging aspects of that job?
4. Why did you leave, where did you go, and why did you choose that next employer?

For candidates who have had previous jobs in sales (and I expect that many of the candidates that you will be interviewing for a sales role *will*), ask them to outline the following for each role and each year:

1. What was your quota, and how did you perform against it?
2. How big was your sales team, and where did you rank in performance?
3. How did your company compete and win in the market? This answer will give you an indication of:
   - how smart they are
   - how well they communicate
   - how well they understood the true value proposition of that employer

Throughout the interview, I always recommend taking detailed notes for later reference (I usually write my notes on a printed copy of their résumé). If the candidate progresses to the next steps of your process, you will need to refer back to some of these notes in later interviews. Writing on their résumé makes it easy to return to the notes when needed.

During the interview, I also like to score the candidate on a simple scale of 1–3 on the attributes our company hires for (intelligence, drive, humility, optimism, and passion). You, of course, may have different attributes, but this scoring helps come decision time—especially because you will have six to ten candidates vying for each sales role. I rough out the chart below on their CV while I'm interviewing them:

Attribute	Score 1–3
Intelligence	
Drive	
Humility	
Passion	
Optimism	

After the first face-to-face interview, be sure to inform the candidate about the next steps in the interview process (if they don't proactively ask about it). You can tell them:

1. You are meeting with several candidates for the first interviews.
2. You will shortlist the group who will make it to the second interview.

3. Everyone will know their status in one week (maximum), and they can email or call anytime if they are looking for a status update or think of any further questions.

As noted, strong candidates will likely be interviewing with multiple companies simultaneously. Out of consideration, they need to know where they stand in your company's interview process so that they can make appropriate decisions about other options they may have at hand. In my experience, too many companies (usually larger ones) show a lack of consideration and are unresponsive to a candidate after they have taken the time and effort to interview for their company.

If you decide against a candidate, let them know as soon as possible so they don't turn down other opportunities with a false expectation of moving forward with your company. Making a career change can be an exciting time. Still, it can also be stressful for some people, so being more communicative with the candidate will reflect positively on your company. For candidates with several potential options, all positive interactions they have with you go a long way.

 Pro Tip: Treat your candidates as you would want to be treated when interviewing. Tell them where they stand in the interviewing process and outline the next steps. Never diminish a candidate's confidence or self-esteem. If you are not going to hire them, fine. But don't damage their confidence for the next interview they are going to.

The business community is a small place. You never know which interview candidate today will become a client or prospect five years from now.

Second Interview: They Present Their Ninety-Day Onboarding Plan

Following the first interview, if you think the candidate is strong enough to progress to the next stage, you will bring them back for Interview 2, the "ninety-day onboarding plan." The basis of this interview is that you will give the candidate "the floor" for the first fifteen to twenty minutes of the second interview and ask them to present a plan of what they would do in the first ninety days if hired by your company. Specifically, what will be their ramp-up plan to learn your business, industry, and how you sell so they can start contributing?

Send them a follow-up email explaining your expectations for the onboarding plan interview. Be sure to make the following clear:

- They can present their plan any way they want.
- You are available if they have questions before the second interview.
- You will give them adequate preparation time (generally at least four to seven days).

Here is a sample email to the new hire candidate following the first phase of the interview process and setting the expectations for the second interview—the ninety-day onboarding plan:

> *Hi Malcolm,*
>
> *Thank you again for your interest in the account executive role at IN THE FUNNEL. It was a pleasure meeting you yesterday.*
>
> *I'm delighted to inform you that we want to move you to the next stage in our interview process!*

> *As discussed, for the next interview, we will give you the "floor" for the first fifteen or twenty minutes so that you can share your onboarding plan for the first ninety days in this role.*
>
> *Specifically, we'd like to know your plan to learn about our business, our clients, and the way we sell to ensure you ramp up quickly.*
>
> *You can present your plan any way you would like.*
>
> *After you present your onboarding plan, we will use the back half of the interview to discuss some items on our list further and make ourselves available for any questions that you might have about the company or the role.*
>
> *Please feel free to reach out with any questions about this whatsoever.*
>
> *Best, Mark*

The ninety-day onboarding plan exercise allows us to assess three things (at a minimum) about the candidate:

How they present an idea: Salespeople must be able to engage an audience and present an idea as part of their core job function. This exercise gives us an early look at the candidate's skill set.

How they research and present a new topic: Most salespeople have not considered this topic, so the subject matter might be new to them. It is interesting to assess how they take on a small project when dealing with some ambiguity (an essential requirement for most new sales-people to be successful in their new companies).

How serious they are about the process and landing the role with your company: This first assignment will be an early indicator of how they will perform if or when you hire them.

I can't tell you how powerful the ninety-day onboarding plan exercise has been in the hiring I have been involved with in recent years.

Several years ago, I was consulting with the leadership team of an amazing financial services company called Open Access. Open Access is an independent provider of group retirement services and employer pension plans. After we completed our ITF Discovery (our initial con-sulting engagement), we determined that we needed to add salespeople to their team.

I worked with the chief operating officer on building and leading the sales team. Together, we interviewed candidates for a new account executive sales role.

One of our tenets at IN THE FUNNEL is that when preparation meets opportunity, good things happen. A candidate named Ryan showed up to present his ninety-day onboarding plan and wowed all of us in the room.

Ryan had sent his onboarding plan to us twenty-four hours in advance, so we knew he had put significant work into it. He presented a very well-thought-out strategic plan that made sense. He explained it to us from the front of the room in PowerPoint with color hard copies for all attendees. Then Ryan did something that blew us all away.

He presented a slide called "Market Feedback" that had not been included in the original package he had sent us. It turns out that Ryan had reached out to five financial advisers to ask them for their impressions of Open Access. The financial planning channel was very important to Open Access.

This was a very high-paying sales leadership job, so Ryan made the right effort to earn it. And earn it, he did. We happily hired Ryan for that role.

Now, eight years later, after an amazingly successful sales and sales-leadership run at Open Access, Ryan Spaulding is the president and CEO of Open Access (and yes, we take credit for all of that).

More food for thought: Back then, we asked Ryan why he accepted the role at Open Access because we knew he was deciding between multiple offers from different financial services firms. Ryan told us that one of the main reasons he decided to come on board was the "first-class interviewing process."

 Pro Tip: Although you ask candidates to prepare an onboarding plan, let them know that your firm has its own disciplined onboarding plan to help ensure their success. Lots more on this in Chapter 8.

How to Get Team Consensus on Hiring Decisions

When multiple people from your organization interview a candidate, one of the challenges you will face is getting a consensus on whether to hire a candidate. Post-interview meetings with your team will become a free-for-all if you aren't careful, so I use the following structure to try to efficiently gather thoughtful feedback from the team before making the decision.

At the end of the interview, ask each of the interviewers to take five minutes to create a written summary of the following:

1. **The three things they liked most about this candidate and why.**
2. **The three things they liked least about this candidate and why.**
3. **Their decision on whether they would move the candidate into the next stage of the process.**

Your goal in using this approach is to have each interviewer thoughtfully consider what they think about the candidate before they are influenced by the opinions of others in the room. This structure also helps people logically organize their thoughts on the candidate before sharing. If they like (or don't like) the candidate, they must understand why.

After five minutes, go around the room and allow everyone to share what they liked, what they didn't like, and whether they would move them to the next stage in the interview process.

After everyone has shared their thoughts, the stage is set for an open discussion. At that point, being influenced by someone else's observations or opinions is OK. Discuss as a group and decide.

It is very common for people to have difficulty deciding. They flip-flop or want to weigh in with an opinion but avoid *making* the decision. Making difficult decisions regarding people is particularly tough if you don't do it regularly...and most entrepreneurs don't hire salespeople on a regular basis. The good news is that this "muscle" improves with reps, so the more you use it, the better you get.

The more candidates you interview, the more your hiring decision team will improve, especially if you have an excellent post-interview process to share feedback in a structured manner.

Remember, sales leaders and business executives are paid to make decisions. So, assess the candidates and make the best decision based on their interview performance.

Offering the Candidate a Sales Job

First, call them (don't email them) and tell them you would like to offer them a job subject to a few reference checks. In this call, share your excitement about your decision and be authentic in your feedback on why you're excited to have them join the team. Assume that they are considering multiple other job offers, so at this point, you are still in *sales mode*—assure them they will have a great future working with your company.

Also, let them know you will prepare an offer letter during the reference check process. Verbally share the compensation, bonus, benefits, and key elements of the offer to come.

I also recommend giving the candidate your calendar availability and asking *them* to schedule the fifteen-minute reference checks with their contacts (it's faster and more efficient for you). Most people erroneously delegate reference checks to someone in human resources or go through the motions and treat it as a rubber stamp. As an entrepreneur or sales leader, I encourage you to make these calls yourself. Most will be overwhelmingly positive about the candidate and won't reveal anything that will change your mind. Still, occasionally, you will hear some information that will be helpful. Be engaged in the call and have a few great questions prepared.

On reference calls, people will be a little more candid if you position a question in the past so that they can provide some helpful information that does not speak ill of the candidate today.

Here's an example of how to start a reference call with a past employer:

> *"Sabrina, thank you so much for taking the time to chat with me today about Paul.*
>
> *We are impressed with Paul; he presented well in our interview process. Paul mentioned that when he worked for you at Salesforce, he had a very tough time getting used to the volume of sales activity required in his first year. Can you tell me more about that?"*

Remember, you asked Paul about the "tougher parts of each role" during your initial interview. You took notes on his résumé and can now reference some of those notes to get more specific on the reference call.

Again, most of the time, the reference calls will be a positive reinforcement of the candidate, but listen carefully and don't hesitate to dig deeper if you sense something might be lurking below the surface of a comment. If nothing else, the insight might help you understand how best to manage Paul in the future while at your company.

The Offer Letter
The offer letter should be short and positive, not corporate, legal, and boring.

You're a sales leader and love your business and customers. Make that enthusiasm contagious and get the candidate excited about joining.

If you are hiring for someone with a performance-based compensation plan (and you should be if it is a sales role), then the offer letter should identify the target income for the position and the split between base salary and the commissionable upside or sales incentive target.

Here's an example of how to address the compensation portion of the offer letter:

> *"Your total target compensation will be $150,000/annum, which includes a base salary of $75,000 plus a commission target of $75,000 per annum, subject to applicable withholdings. The company's ordinary payroll procedures will pay your salary on the 15th and the last day of each month."*

Generally, there is no need to provide a detailed sales incentive (commission) plan at the offer letter phase of the hiring process. Sales incentive plans are generally subject to change. In most cases, the candidate you are hiring will not have enough context on your business and the industry to assess the detailed comp plan before hiring anyway, so don't confuse them with it or create an unnecessary objection without need.

Send the offer letter to the candidate quickly and give a reasonable time frame for them to return it signed (generally within four to seven days).

Once you have successfully hired your preferred candidate, your focus should be on ensuring an efficient and effective ramp-up and orientation so you can minimize the time it takes them to start providing value to your company.

Now, let's discuss what the formal onboarding plan should look like for a new sales hire to maximize the odds of them becoming a productive and permanent member of your team.

CHAPTER SUMMARY

- Recruiting productive, permanent salespeople is one of the most difficult jobs in business.
- Before interviewing candidates, document what you are looking for in a detailed job description, including success metrics for the first three, six, and nine months.
- There are four steps to an effective interview process for a salesperson:
    a. screening interview (video or live)
    b. top-grading interview
    c. ninety-day onboarding plan review
    d. reference checks
- Live telephone reference checks should be completed by the hiring manager (not HR).
- Read *Who* by Geoff Smart and Randy Street.
- Before interviewing candidates, agree on who from your firm will be involved in deciding and who will make the final decision.
- Remember the Golden Rule—always treat interview candidates as you would like to be treated.
- Make sure that your company has a documented onboarding plan to reduce the time to value for the new sales hire.

Chapter 8

THE NEW SALES HIRE
ONBOARDING PLAN

We've all been there.

You get hired by a company for a role that looks tremendously exciting. You take two weeks off before joining, and the anticipation builds.
On your first day at the new job, you arrive early at the office and
discover that almost nothing has been prepared for your arrival. It's
a massive letdown.

I have lived through several very disappointing first days on the job.
Here are a couple examples.

On my first day in my second professional job as an account executive
at a large, privately held company, I discovered that there was no desk,
no computer, and nobody in the organization was even aware that a
new *hotshot* salesperson named Mark Cox was supposed to be starting
that day! This was a poor start at a pretty good company.

I arrived to start a new role as a senior vice president of sales for a $500
million-plus company, and I was relegated to working from a vacant

desk in the bullpen for the first couple of weeks while the person that I was replacing worked out his final two weeks in my office. Talk about awkward! The CEO visited me on the first day and was "disappointed" to see my temporary workspace but didn't do anything about it. This was a poor start at a company with an awful culture. I left soon after I started.

I have also had an amazing first day on the job.

In my first corporate job ever, I arrived at the office to meet five other new sales hires who were starting the same day as me. We were introduced to our incredibly well-structured, well-organized three-month onboarding program. Walking into the meeting room dedicated to our new hire team for our onboarding program, we saw our laptops, business cards, company swag, onboarding binders, and detailed ninety-day agendas laid carefully on the table. We were greeted by the dedicated sales-enablement onboarding manager, who spent each day working with us in the first six weeks. In the seventh week, we all traveled to the company's Marketing Education Center (most often referred to as *Sales University*) in Rochester, New York. At Sales University, we dove deep into the products and processes with experts within the business.

By the end of the training and orientation program (day ninety-one), every new hire in my group was unbelievably well prepared for the first day on the job in front of customers and prospects. The onboarding plan for a new sales hire in this organization was so good that executive recruiters would approach new sales hires when they had finished the training to offer them higher-paying roles with other companies, even though they had not yet sold a thing. This company did it right.

Although I may be dating myself a bit here, the third example was back in 1993, when companies like Xerox, IBM, Kodak, and Motorola would invest thousands of dollars in training new sales hires (I started with Kodak, and their onboarding plan was amazing). As a result, the competition for these roles was fierce, and getting hired was extremely difficult. I received an opportunity only because a buddy of mine was working there and got my application in front of the right people.

New grads like me knew that if you got hired by one of these companies, the new-hire onboarding program was a formal sales certification on your résumé for life and could be as powerful as your degree (kind of like the IN THE FUNNEL Professional Sales certification badge on your LinkedIn profile). When I received a phone call in December of 1992 from their friendly HR professional advising me that I had been hired, I felt like I had won the lottery. Fun note: thirty years later, I still remember where I was for that life-changing telephone call.

Of course, I'm not advocating that your company set up a state-of-the-art marketing education center to use for new sales hires, but you can still knock the socks off your new team members by showing them that you are taking an active role in their success with your company.

An effective onboarding program can help minimize the chances of having a salesperson or any new hire flounder in your company, increase their chances of success, and accelerate their "time to value" by smoothing out their learning curve.

> *Beginnings have a far greater impact than most of us understand. Beginnings, in fact, can matter to the end.*[25] —Daniel Pink

New Sales Hire Onboarding Plan Objectives

To maximize the new sales hire's chances of success, you need to deliver a formal onboarding program with the following objectives:

- **To ensure the new sales hire becomes a productive, successful, permanent team member.**
- **To decrease the time required for the new sales hire to start selling well.**
- **To establish milestones to provide the new sales hire with real-time feedback on their performance and progress during their onboarding period.**

Pre-Start-Date Setup

The pre-start-date planning and activities will show your new sales hires how important they are to your company and the investment you have made in their success. We suggest that as soon as possible after receiving the signed offer letter from your successful candidate, you send them the following:

- Reference materials for them to review before their start date (presentations, proposals, product information, press releases, etc.). It's best to share public domain information because you will have a small percentage of sales hires who accept an offer, sign an offer letter, and then back out before joining your company. In these (hopefully) rare instances, you don't want confidential information like your go-to-market strategy or detailed compensation plan to be in their possession.
- A copy of the book *The First 90 Days* by Michael Watkins. This is an excellent read on strategies to reduce "time to value" for new employees.

 A copy of your formal onboarding plan. Download our simple onboarding plan template here: https://www.inthefunnel.com/ltls-sales-tools *Password: thesellingwell*

- If you have them, send them company-branded gifts
  such as a coffee mug, a mouse pad, or a company T-shirt.
  As simple as it seems, everyone loves swag!

As a new hire, imagine your impression of your new employer upon receiving this material soon after being hired!

Sending them the new-hire onboarding plan lets them know how seriously you are taking this process, but it also gives them a sense of the level of work required to succeed. Schedule a thirty-minute call to walk them through the onboarding plan.

Also, as part of the pre-start-date setup:

- Distribute a company announcement about the new
  sales hire two weeks before their arrival and be sure to
  cc them. The announcement should explain who they
  are, what they will be doing for your firm, and why you
  hired them. Ask the candidate to help with their bio. The
  idea is to set them up for success before joining and put
  some wind in their sails.
- Ensure that the new hire's environment is ready *before*
  their first day—this includes their desk, laptop, mobile
  device, email, passwords, and system logins for your
  various technology platforms.
- Make the new hire aware that they should be prepared
  to introduce themselves to their peers on their first day.

Day 1: Orientation
After preparing so well for the big day during the pre-start-day setup, you can now focus on showing the new hire the ropes. Remember, first impressions matter.

Day 1 for the new sales hire must include (at a minimum) the following:

- a detailed review of the sales plan or sales playbook by you, the entrepreneur/founder/sales leader
- HR orientation (office tour, payroll and benefits overview, security passes, rules, etc.)
- meet-and-greets with key executives in your company
- a walking tour of the office with introductions to the whole team
- a detailed review of the ninety-day onboarding plan

Field Fast Start Program

Every aspect of the onboarding process is essential, but the "field fast start" is the most critical.

Within ninety days of joining the company, the new sales hire must develop knowledge in three domains to position themselves for success:

1. **Your company,** including the business strategy, organizational structure, people, processes in place, and technologies they will need to use
2. **The Ideal Customer Profiles** that you sell to, including industries and buying personas
3. **How you sell** (your sales process, sales strategy, and buyer's journey)

Each week during the onboarding program, the new hire will be given content to study, practical exposure to clients, and feedback on their progress.

A natural cadence that has worked well for many companies I have worked with is to provide the content and practical exposure during the week, with a scheduled presentation by the new hire to select onboarding team members at the end of each week. Communicating this cadence to the new hires will set them up for success as they plan for each week's activities.

 Pro Tip: Set up all internal meetings for the new sales hire with your team in advance versus expecting them to chase all the different players to get time on their calendar. Also, if someone is meeting with a new sales hire, they must be coached on how to effectively run the meeting versus just having a "coffee catch-up."

Over six weeks, the new sales hire will be expected to present on the following topics:

1. Your company (ten-minute intro as if presented to a new prospect)
2. Your customers and industries that you sell to, including your ICP and buyer personas
3. Your solutions (including demos or walk-throughs)
4. Key competitors and what makes you unique and different
5. How you sell, your sales playbook
6. Draft 1.0 of their *territory game plan*
   - You'll want to understand how they will prioritize pursuing your target market and what activity and objective KPIs (key performance indicators) they will achieve.
   - Their first draft will need your input, but they will be more committed to it because *they* created it, rather than you.

Depending on the nature of your business, these topics can be modified slightly, but this list works for companies in most industries within a B2B or solution sales environment.

During their onboarding program, you must also expose the new sales hire to your prospects and customers (with supervision). There is no better way for them to learn than by hearing about the problems your customers may be experiencing and what your business can offer to solve them.

Evaluation Milestones

Within the field fast start program, the new sales hire will have a weekly one-on-one with their sales leader. The expectation of a weekly presentation will provide an excellent outlet for immediate and relevant feedback during these sessions.

When one of the new hire's presentations does not meet expectations, these one-on-one sessions are the perfect venue to provide constructive, immediate feedback. The beauty of having these prescheduled on the calendar is that the new hire expects it—it's just *part of the program.*

Remember, one of the main objectives of the onboarding plan is to expose the new sales hire to the authentic culture of your company and sales team. Don't hide it. For now, your culture is what it is, and for the new hire to be successful, they need to understand it. Feedback is the breakfast of champions, so be prepared to provide them with authentic coaching during the onboarding process, and you will establish the expectation for weekly one-on-ones moving forward.

When we were consulting with PureFacts Financial Solutions (reminder, they are a revenue management SaaS offering for wealth management), we decided to expand their sales team. We worked with them to recruit, interview, hire, and onboard some great salespeople.

We followed the onboarding strategies and tactics to the letter so that the organization valued and welcomed each new sales hire. The new hires might have even felt too comfortable because of our efforts.

As part of their onboarding program, two new hires were scheduled to present a fifteen-minute corporate overview, inclusive of a value proposition. Everything up to that point had been pleasant, cheerful, and courteous.

When presenting their corporate overviews to me and a few executive team members on the Friday of their first week, they advised that they would do it together (versus individually), which was not what we expected. They did the presentation sitting down and a little bit casually as if they were peers chatting with us during lunch versus what we expected: a customer role-play.

This was a letdown for us, and we immediately shared our feedback (in a positive professional way). We clarified that they were underprepared and took the presentation a bit too casually. We told them that wasn't how we did things at PureFacts and that we expected a significantly better effort next week when they redid the presentation. Although they were both taken aback a little by the direct feedback, we saw an extremely professional, effective corporate overview presentation one week later that impressed everyone in the room.

One of those initial sales hires is still with PureFacts as their sales leader (eight years later), and we often look back and laugh about that incident. As of today, he is one of the best SaaS enterprise salespeople in North America that we have ever worked with.

It is important to emphasize that the one-on-ones with new sales hires are meant to be a two-way dialogue. In addition to receiving your feedback, it's also an opportunity for the new hire to share how things are going from their perspective. Make them feel comfortable sharing with you what is working, what is not, and what support they need to succeed during their onboarding.

The Final Milestone

Before the new sales hires are unleashed on their territory, they must create and present their quarterly sales plan to the executive or sales team. This strategic and tactical plan should include weekly goals and objectives for demand-generation activities, approach calls, and sales-funnel development. This plan can also be the reference for future one-on-ones to evaluate their progress.

After they complete their onboarding program, ask for feedback on improving it for the next hire. Continuous improvement is the name of the game in onboarding. The better we are at this, the faster our new sales hires can start driving revenue for the business.

Implementing this onboarding approach in your business will take time and effort, but I promise you that the results you will see and the disruption you will avoid will be well worth the investment.

Once you have built your sales team, you must lead, coach, and manage them to accelerate the growth of your business. That's the focus of Part 3: how to actively coach, motivate, and inspect the sales team.

CHAPTER SUMMARY

- A formal onboarding plan is one of the critical success factors for a new sales hire.
- The purpose of the onboarding plan is to educate the new hire on your company, the ICP you sell to, and how you sell.
- The onboarding plan has several stages, starting weeks before the new hire's first day.
- Treat the program as a formal certification, with some criteria to "graduate."
- The direct manager and the new hire are jointly responsible for successful onboarding.
- First impressions really matter. They will take the onboarding plan as seriously as you do, so be prepared.

Part 3

LEAD YOUR
SALES TEAM

Chapter 9

SALES LEADER: THE HARDEST ROLE IN BUSINESS

It should have been the best professional year of my life. I had just turned thirty-two, and after working as a high-performing salesperson in three separate companies, I was finally promoted to director of sales and put in charge of seven salespeople. I was now responsible for the revenue of the entire division.

This was a tough job to get, as the guy running the sales organization was amazing, and he had recruited some of the best salespeople in the business.

He moved "up," and I moved into my dream job as a sales leader for the first time in the corporate world.

Four months later, everyone on the sales team was unhappy, including me. I was miserable at work for the first time in my career. My sales team was underperforming big time, and I was not helping. I couldn't understand why everyone couldn't just do the job the same way I had done it when I was the top sales rep in the company.

I'd cut my management teeth about ten years prior when I was managing student painting franchises for a company called Student Works Painting. In this role, I recruited very green students and, in six months, helped them go from zero business experience to operating their own profitable painting company with a team of six to eight painters under them. The growth I helped these students achieve was astounding, and they loved the coaching and leadership I provided. In addition, I *loved* coaching them and seeing them grow. What was different now in this corporate environment?

The difference was my mindset. When managing the students with the painting company, I knew that my role as a leader was to trust and inspire them to achieve their potential by creating a supportive environment. I saw these students as entrepreneurs and I understood that they were in charge of their businesses, and I was their coach.

In the corporate assignment, I had unknowingly defaulted to a "command and control" leadership style. I was managing the team to hit my goals as their leader. My focus was on me and my goals versus them and their growth. This approach diminished the team's autonomy, creativity, and fun.

The corporate sales management assignment became so unpleasant that I seriously considered leaving the company to take another direct contributor (nonmanagement) sales role. This would have been a disastrous step back in my career. My confidence in my ability to manage salespeople was shattered.

Sales management is by far the most challenging job in business. According to Manny Medina, Max Altschuler, and Mark Kosoglow in their book *Sales Engagement,* the average tenure for a VP of sales has been steadily declining from twenty-six months (in 2010) to nineteen months (in 2017).[26] This means that the average sales leader lasts fewer than two years in their job before being fired or leaving on their own. What's worse, entrepreneurs can't "leave." They often struggle for years leading the sales team with no systems, processes, or tools.

Sales leadership is a very difficult thing to figure out organically. For this chapter, I will refer to anyone in a sales management role (entrepreneur, CEO, chief revenue officer, VP, director, or manager) as a *sales leader* or *sales manager*.

This chapter is also intended to provide salespeople with insight into the sales leader's role so:

1. They will have empathy for what their leaders are going through
2. They can understand who best to help and support their leaders to succeed
3. They can learn what they will face when they progress to a sales leadership position

Why Is Sales Management So Hard?

Sales leaders answer to the three most demanding stakeholders in business: customers, the executive team/board of directors, and the sales team. All three critically important stakeholders have ever-increasing demands on your time and incredibly high expectations.

The role of sales leaders itself is incredibly broad. This table highlights just some of the responsibilities of a sales leader today.

Meet revenue growth targets profitably.	Acquire new customers and grow revenue from existing customers.
Build the sales strategy.	Determine whom we will target and how we will win.
Build the team.	Recruit, onboard, train, and motivate the sales team.
Ensure the adoption of a standard sales process.	Optimize the sales process to maximize efficiency and productivity.
Enable the team.	Further the team's growth with professional sales training, technology, and tools.
Stay market competitive.	Monitor market trends, understand customer needs, and develop strategies to differentiate your products and services in the marketplace.
Accurately forecast and plan.	Allocate resources and budget and forecast the annual sales plan.
Build the right sales tech stack and ensure adoption.	Select the appropriate sales tech stack for the business and ensure proper adoption.

The role of a sales leader today is so broad that you must be a massively talented chameleon to succeed. A successful sales leader is part cheerleader, drill sergeant, strategist, data scientist, behavioral scientist, psychologist, and technologist.

The issue that further compounds the difficulty in the sales leadership role is that the sales leader has the most black-and-white measurements of professional success: sales numbers. You either hit your monthly/quarterly/annual sales goals or you don't. This is unlike any other role on the leadership team (marketing, product, operations, finance) because your core success metric is always on public display. The sales scoreboard is in the public domain throughout the company.

OK, it's a tough job, for sure. In some cases, it can be the worst job in the company...but it also has the potential to be the best. In my experience, three things determine whether entrepreneurs or corporate sales leaders hate or love their roles as sales leaders:

- **the sales culture**
- **the sales team**
- **your sales management system**

The excellent news is that, as a sales leader, you are in control of all three.

The Sales Culture

Before building a sales team (or even a company), you must start by deciding on the type of sales culture you want for the organization. *Merriam-Webster Dictionary* defines "culture" as "the set of shared attitudes, values, goals, and practices that characterize an institution or organization." I often simplify this further: culture is how *we do things around here*.

Pro Tip: If you want to create an intentional culture in your business or sales team, start by identifying the core values you want the team to showcase.

The starting point is naming the values you want the team to showcase daily, and explaining why you want those values embedded in your organization. Once you have identified the values, you can use them as a guide when:

- working with customers and prospects
- collaborating with your team
- leading your sales team
- considering new salespeople to join the team

At IN THE FUNNEL, we have identified the following values to drive our culture:

ITF Core Value	Why
Customer First	We must ensure that everything we do provides enormous value to our customers.
Accountability	We do what we say we will do.
Integrity	No need for a "why" here…this is self-evident.
Drive for Results	Performance matters.
Lifelong Learning	We are growth-oriented—we invest in our professional development and learning.

| Fun | We want to enjoy ourselves while doing great work. |
| Commitment | We showcase discipline and perseverance to adhere to all other values identified here. |

Keeping the list reasonably short is difficult, but the shorter the list, the better the chance your team has of remembering and internalizing it. Complexity is always the enemy of execution. We suggest engaging the sales team in identifying the culture's core values with this exercise.

Exercise: Build the core values for the team.

Set up a forty-five-minute meeting on this topic and ask everyone on the sales team to name the five to seven values they think should be the foundation of the sales culture and why. Have them come to the meeting prepared to share in five minutes or less. You might even circulate a sample list of twenty or thirty values to choose from (like the following list).

Loyalty	Respect	Excellence	Work–Life Balance
Intelligence	Generosity	Innovation	Compassion
Creativity	Honesty	Speed	Professionalism
Success	Teamwork	Courage	Relationship
Gratitude	Customer First	Patience	Reciprocity
Adaptability	Diversity and Inclusion	Community Engagement	Sustainability

Pro Tip: For a broader list of potential values to consider, ask ChatGPT for the "Top fifty cultural values showcased by great companies."

Consider the sales team's responses as you refine and land on the final list. The team will feel more connected and committed to the culture and values if they help create them. To make your values real, you need to live them. For example, if one of the values is accountability, you must hold your team accountable (compassionately). If customer first is a core value, you must always showcase a customer-first mentality, even if that means doing something challenging or negatively impacting your bottom line.

Clarifying the specific sales culture you want to create will be helpful as you work with the existing team and recruit new salespeople.

The Sales Team

The key takeaway from this section is that as a sales leader, you choose who is on the team. And yes, the same applies if you have just taken on the role of managing an existing team.

As a sales leader, if someone is not the right fit for the team, replace them. Looking back, one of the errors that I made (on more occasions than I care to count) was taking too long to replace someone who was not a good fit.

If someone isn't the right fit for your sales team, it's not just their personal performance that suffers. A wrong-fit teammate ripples throughout the organization and negatively impacts the sales culture itself. This is particularly true if they have long tenures. The ripple effect works positively and negatively.

How can you tell if it's a problem or a blip? No matter how good they are, any salesperson will have good and bad months, quarters, and even years. In the same way, going back to my sports analogy, it's rare that any professional athlete has a great game every time they take the field. It is also important to highlight that performance varies. Sometimes, this happens for reasons within our control and sometimes for reasons outside our control (think back to the COVID-19 pandemic). Because of this, you cannot always look at the numbers to determine who stays and who goes.

My filter for determining whether someone is the right or wrong fit for the team is simple: *Performance*: Are they hitting their goals? *Values*: Do they exhibit the attitude we want on our sales team?

Team Assessment Matrix

	PERFORMANCE	VALUES
Star	Yes	Yes
Coachable	No	Yes
Trouble	Yes	No
Wrong Fit	No	No

If someone is hitting their goals (performing) and showcasing the core values you want in your sales culture, they are a star. Alternatively, someone who is not performing and does not exhibit the core values is also an easy decision—they are a *wrong* fit. The more difficult decisions come when assessing someone in the other two categories, coachable and trouble.

If someone is not hitting their goals and activity levels (not performing) but *does* showcase the core values you want as part of your sales culture, they should stay as long as they are *coachable* because this means they can move in the right direction. In my experience, having a growth orientation or being coachable must be inherent in all members of a strong sales team. However, this is particularly important for someone who still needs to improve to hit their goals. If the underperforming individual is not coachable, they cannot develop and will not improve, meaning they are a *wrong fit*.

If a salesperson is performing but not displaying the core values you want on the sales team, they are *trouble* and not fit for the long term. You may need to be a little strategic on the timing of a change depending on their tenure, relationships with customers, and the status of your sales team's performance for the year. Still, if they do not exhibit the values of your sales culture, they will eventually need to go.

If this person has tenure and experience, they may become highly influential to new sales hires (even if you don't intend this to happen). New sales hires will mimic the established team member's negative behaviors and attitudes, and their values may morph in the same direction over time. New salespeople often assume that if the experienced salesperson has lasted this long in the company, they must know what they are doing and be highly regarded by leadership. After all, why wouldn't they think that? It's a logical assumption that if the company were not pleased with this individual's performance and behavior, they would not employ them.

Another side effect of keeping team members around who do not display the values you want on the sales team is that their influence over other team members may diminish your authority as the sales leader. Disruptive team members negatively affect your ability to manage a motivated team of aligned and engaged individuals.

The bottom line is that your sales team needs to adhere to the values you want to be showcased in your sales team and your company, whether or not they are performing.

 Pro Tip: Trust your gut. If you don't look forward to one-on-one meetings with members of your sales team, they are likely not a good fit for the culture or company.

The Sales Management System

Once you have a sales team in place that is living the values that contribute to your sales culture, what do you need to focus on as a sales leader to help them achieve consistent, double-digit sales growth?

Your job as a sales leader is to influence the future behaviors of the sales team in a positive way.

Here are the three things you can do as a sales leader to positively influence the sales team's future behaviors:

- **Inspect the team.**
- **Motivate the team.**
- **Coach the team.**

Let's look at each of these individually.

Inspect the Team

The numbers matter in business, period. Revenue, profit, growth, churn...all these metrics measure the health of your business at any given point in time for your stakeholders. For entrepreneurs, these metrics determine whether your business survives.

We need to grow and be profitable to exist as businesses, so in your role as a sales leader, you need to understand how the team is performing against your objectives. However, sales results are just one indicator. As sales leaders, you also need to look at the sales *activities* that lead to sales objectives that lead to sales results. Knowing that someone either hit or missed their sales goal is not enough. And often, when you realize this has occurred, it's too late. You need to know *why* they missed the number so that you can leverage that information to coach their behaviors and performance in the future.

 Pro Tip: Sales activities lead to sales objectives that lead to sales results. You have lots of control over sales activities (e.g., reaching out to new prospects) but less control over sales objectives (e.g., getting to meet with that prospect for a sales call or providing them a proposal for some business), and even less control over results (e.g., whether they purchase the solution). Focus your sales team on all three metrics.

Suppose Tami missed her quarterly sales results but exceeded every activity target she set for herself, like outreach, approach calls, and proposals. As a sales leader, you must focus on managing results and activity. If she is doing the activity and missing results, perhaps she needs coaching on some aspect of selling.

One of the most significant issues I consistently see with ineffective sales leaders is that they focus too much of their time and effort on inspection, ignoring the other two core responsibilities: motivation and coaching. They look in the rearview mirror of their CRM system and identify performance gaps across sales activities, objectives, and results. Inspection is only *part* of your job as a sales leader; frankly, it's easy.

Motivate the Team

If you're a sales leader, you were likely one of the top salespeople on the team before moving into management. Sales roles require intelligence, tenacity, courage, vulnerability, resilience, and perseverance. The brutal reality of the professional sales role is that we will all come up against massive amounts of rejection and failure throughout our careers. Being mindful of this in your role as a sales leader is essential. The day-to-day challenges in professional sales are different and, in many cases, tougher than in other roles within your organization.

There are times to show salespeople some tough love to drive enhanced performance, but there are other times to show them *love*. Help them, support them, encourage them. Notice them doing something great and call it out.

Also know that different things motivate different people. Not all professional salespeople are driven by the almighty dollar (although some are!). Other factors drive many salespeople, including personal and professional growth, mastery, recognition, autonomy, and competition. Of course, money matters, but as a sales leader, one of the most important things you can learn about each one of your sales team members is what motivates them specifically.

Pro Tip: To truly understand what drives your salespeople, you need to understand why they work and why they work for your company. As simple as this sounds, just asking these questions of your sales team will improve your working relationships.

An old saying goes, "The team needs to know that you care before they care what you know." Empathy is essential in professional sales and sales leadership.

Here's an example of the power of recognition—or what I refer to as the best $185 I have ever spent.

At IN THE FUNNEL, we often play the role of a fractional chief revenue officer until our customer's business scales to the point of needing a dedicated individual in that position or until we have coached the entrepreneur to play that role.

In one engagement, we worked with a fantastic company, Sunview Patio Doors (now the Novatech Group), that designed, manufactured, and sold patio doors to distributors and builders across North America. They were an industry leader with an excellent sales team of experienced and newer sales reps. The company had a great culture emanating from its president, Tony Margiotta, a strategic, growth-oriented leader.

After about ninety days of working together, we had put together a fantastic sales playbook built for their business, and we were running the sales team with a solid sales management system. I spent a day on-site every two weeks for what we called "sales day," consisting of group sales meetings, one-on-one sessions with each sales rep, and some sales training initiatives.

After some initial resistance to me as a consultant (which was understandable), the sales team committed to learning our approach to selling. Our involvement also triggered growth orientation among team members who had been doing the job for so long that certain aspects had become routine.

This is where my $185 investment came in.

In one group sales meeting at the tail end of the third quarter, I announced that I would create two annual awards for the team. My lifelong nickname among friends is Coxy. In this vein, I decided these awards would (somewhat jokingly) be called "the Coxys." My announcement amused the team, and I told them that I would be purchasing the Coxy trophies out of my pocket, and they would be awarded to the top sales rep (as measured by the percentage of quota achieved) and the most improved sales rep.

When I announced it, I threw it out in the meeting without much pre-planning and thought it might contribute a few laughs at our year-end lunch. What I had not planned on was the Coxys driving a massive amount of engagement relative to my meager investment.

For the next four months, the team drove harder than ever to win the coveted Coxys, and unprompted, reps would mention the awards in group meetings or one-on-ones. Even when they referenced it in jest, it was top of mind. It's incredible how competition can drive results.

Even when certain salespeople had already exceeded their annual quotas, they kept pushing hard right until the last day of the year to win one of these trophies and maintain bragging rights for the following year.

We ended up running the Coxy program for three years in the company, and the trophies were proudly displayed as permanent fixtures on the desks of the winners. Recognition not only matters, but it also motivates!

 Pro Tip: The joy in being a sales leader comes from unleashing the true potential of your salespeople and seeing them grow. If this is not something you enjoy, don't become a sales leader.

Coach the Team

The primary way that professional salespeople improve their mindsets and skill sets is through effective coaching. According to psychologist Daniel Goleman's *Harvard Business Review* article "Leadership That Gets Results," six basic leadership styles exist. Coaching was one of the styles he explored and was shown to have a "markedly positive" impact on performance. Unfortunately, his article also indicated that many leaders do not have time for the "slow and tedious work of teaching people and helping them grow."[27]

Most of us confuse telling with coaching. Coaching is the process by which sales leaders intentionally facilitate conversations with team members to identify ways to elevate professional performance. This is *not* telling them what to do to close the next deal.

Our job as coaches is to make our team better, not to show that we are the smartest people in the room by telling them what to do. According to Liz Wiseman in her amazing book *Multipliers*, "some leaders seem to drain the intelligence and capability out of the people around them. Their focus on their own intelligence and their resolve to be the smartest person in the room has a diminishing effect on everyone else."[28]

I always think of it this way: If our *real* job as sales leaders is to influence the sales team's future behaviors positively, how else can we do it? Counting past sales activities and results against goals alone will not improve your team's performance in the future. A sales leader's core job is to elevate future sales performance, and the way to do that is through coaching.

Here are a couple of ways to boost your coaching:

Set up specific coaching events (not inspections), in which both you and the team member know it's a coaching session. This could be time in the field in front of a prospect or time sitting together in the office doing demand-generation calls.

Use the following framework (assess, question, align) to avoid telling people what to do:

- **Assess the situation.**
- **Ask them questions to lead them to understanding the situation.**
- **Align on the go-forward plan.**

The next chapter will focus on the sales management system that enables you to dedicate the time and attention to do those things that matter most as a sales leader.

CHAPTER SUMMARY

- Sales leader is the most challenging role on any executive team.
- Three things make the sales leader role the best or worst job in the company:
    - the sales culture
    - the sales team
    - your sales management system
- In order to create the sales culture you want, name the values you want your team to showcase.
    - Go further by having the team contribute to naming the values.
- The joy of sales leadership comes from unleashing the true potential within salespeople.

Chapter 10

THE ITF SALES MANAGEMENT SYSTEM

As sales leaders, we are pulled in a dozen directions. We are busy and getting busier. Given that growth is critical to every business's success and rests on our shoulders, we must ensure that we give ourselves the best chances of success.

To this end, sales leaders need a reliable sales management system that supports the sales team and drives top-tier performance. You cannot be a successful sales leader by running around putting out fires and being reactive; you need to systematize how you lead the team. An effective sales management system takes the three core activities of sales leaders—to inspect, to motivate, to coach—and puts a framework around them so that you can dedicate the appropriate time, attention, and focus to each one.

As Evan Smith from Berenson, Inc., told us, "I knew the *'what'* of sales leadership, which was trying to help them elevate their performance. I didn't know *how* to most effectively do that. After each set of sales meetings, I was the one who walked away with a ton of action items while the sales team kept doing what they were doing. As an entrepreneur and CEO, I am simply too busy to have every person on my sales team 'up' delegating action items to me. It has the potential to become overwhelming quickly."

Without a sales management system, most sales managers will fall into reactive mode and field whatever comes their way, like an overworked customer service rep who keeps answering service calls with another five people waiting. We see this frequently with sales leaders who say they have an "open door policy." This is another way of saying, "I have no system whatsoever and simply respond to whatever each sales rep thinks is important when they think it's important." This ad-hoc approach rarely improves the sales team, and what's worse is that it quickly burns out the sales leader.

You need a system to keep yourself on track and accountable. More importantly, the system allows you to manage your energy, enthusiasm, and mindset to be your "best self" when working with your sales team versus being tired, grumpy, distracted, or inward-focused.

Intellectually, I don't think anyone will argue with me on this point. Most people will also say that diet and exercise are essential for mental and physical well-being, but they don't exercise enough and overindulge in food that is killing them. Knowing the right things to do and then doing them are very different.

According to sales consultancy Miller Heiman (now Korn Ferry), most sales managers spend twice as much time on administration and forecasting (34.1 percent) as they do on coaching (14.2 percent).[29] Of course, administration and forecasting have absolutely no impact on improving the sales team's performance. Both functions are automated anyway, so why spend time on them?

You need a sales management system to ensure you spend enough time doing the most important things to elevate the sales team's future performance.

Let's dive into our sales management system to help you focus on the most critical aspects of your job as a sales leader. This sales management system of structured meetings and events will ensure that you are being deliberate in your approach and doing what you need to do to be successful and maximize the performance and potential of your sales teams.

These are the essential elements of an effective sales management system:

- one-on-one meetings
- team sales meetings
- time in the field coaching
- big deal reviews
- win/loss reviews
- quarterly sales kickoffs

The One-on-One Meeting

The one-on-one sales meeting focuses on reviewing the progress of a sales rep's game plan for maximizing revenue growth from their territories.

In a nutshell, they are the salesperson's opportunity to convince the sales leader that they have a solid plan to achieve or exceed sales goals for the upcoming period. The structured and disciplined format I have laid out here guides them to think about what they have been doing, document what they plan to do over the coming weeks and months, and then say it out loud, which helps them commit to the plan of action.

Many salespeople won't always exceed the goals or quotas in each period. That is OK. However, they do need a plan to improve performance in the next period, and that's what we are trying to get them to (i) develop, (ii) share, and (iii) align with us.

One-on-One Meeting Summary

Objective	<ul><li>Assess the performance year/quarter/month to date.</li><li>Align on the go-forward plan to elevate sales performance</li><li>Drive accountability to ensure the execution of the plan.</li><li>Provide guidance and support to help the sales rep execute their plan.</li></ul>
Agenda	<ul><li>The Numbers:<ul><li>performance versus quota year-to-date</li><li>committed deals—those that will close during the following period (with 75+ percent certainty)</li><li>upside deals—deals that will close, but timing is less certain)</li></ul></li><li>Top of Funnel Review: what new opportunities have been added recently?</li><li>Current Customers' Health Checks: with which current customers has the rep prioritized a health check meeting?</li><li>New Logos: with which new logos will the salesperson intentionally try to earn an approach call?</li></ul>
Desired Outcomes	<ul><li>The salesperson has developed an effective game plan for the next period.</li><li>Both the sales leader and the salesperson are aligned on the plan.</li><li>The sales rep is committed to their plan.</li></ul>

Pro Tip: Before the one-on-one, assess how the salesperson is doing, develop some great questions to help them understand how they are doing, and aim to align on the go-forward game plan that THEY come up with.

As sales leaders, you must leverage these meetings to collaborate with the salesperson on what to do in the next period to succeed. You cannot simply tell a sales team member what to do if you want their genuine buy-in. The "command and control" leadership style is long gone, and we, as sales leaders, need to be much more intentional and collaborative on how to lead the team.

That's why I suggest that you circulate the standardized agenda for these meetings, so everyone is well aware of the consistent structure of the meeting.

The salesperson will then submit their specific plan *at least* twenty-four hours before the one-on-one. This gives the salesperson time to honestly think about where they are and what needs to be done to improve, and it gives you, as the sales leader, time to assess where the salesperson is at and properly prepare for the one-on-one.

We all think we are good at improvisation, but if we truly were, we'd be stand-up comics at Second City. In addition to playing in a huge rock band and being a professional hockey goalie, this is a lifelong dream of mine and probably the only one that is still a possibility, aside from the unfortunate fact that I'm not funny.

Here's a simple framework to prepare for the meeting:

1. Assess

    a. How are they doing?

    b. What's working and not working?

    c. What are the two or three things you suggest to help improve their performance?

2. Question

    a. What questions will help them analyze and determine some opportunities to improve performance?

3. Align

    a. Once you have had a thoughtful discussion about their situation and discussed some opportunities to improve performance, you can then agree and align on the specific next steps for the period before your next one-on-one.

After the one-on-one meeting, ask the salesperson to send an email summary of what you agreed to as next steps. The leader and the salesperson will also reference this summary before the following one-on-one.

 Pro Tip: *"The biggest single problem with communication is the illusion that it has taken place."*
—George Bernard Shaw

Remember: nobody wants to be told what to do by a boss. Most of the time, your salespeople want to develop the plan they execute. It's better because if they create the plan, they will be more committed to achieving it. When they ask you, "What do you think I should do?" try challenging them with, "Well, I have a couple of ideas, but first, what do *you* think you should do?"

So if, for example, you were to assess that with one salesperson, they did not have enough sales opportunities in their funnel, it's more effective to get them to come to that realization than simply saying, "You need to do more demand generation."

Perhaps the following conversation and questions might be a more effective approach to driving the right behaviors:

> *Mark (sales leader): Hey John, it looks like we are currently slightly behind our sales goals. What might be the best plan to rectify that in the next month or two?*
>
> *John (salesperson): I'm not sure, Mark. I've been working super hard, and the deal with The Hoxton company is taking up a ton of my time.*
>
> *Mark (sales leader): Yeah, I can see that, John, and by the way, great work on that one. I can really see the impact of your attention to detail on that one. Let me ask you this: Do you think the challenge we are having is filling the top of the funnel with new deals, or working and closing the deals in your funnel?*

John (salesperson): Well, I think probably the former, filling the top of the funnel. Once we get a deal in the process, I seem to be good at working it through to sign and I enjoy that process more. The Hoxton deal is an excellent example of that.

Mark (sales leader): Yes, it sure is! OK, if you think the issue is filling the top of the funnel, what is the game plan to try to fill the top of the funnel?

John (salesperson): I'm not sure, Mark. I guess there are a few things I could try. I know that you're a bit of an expert at demand generation, Mark; what do you think I should do?

Mark (sales leader): Thanks, John, that's nice of you to say. I might have a couple of ideas, but first, what do you think you should do?

John (salesperson): Well...when I get down to doing demand generation, I'm pretty good at it. Perhaps if I focused a little more time on it, I might be able to make some progress in the next two to four weeks.

Mark (sales leader): YES! You are good at it, John. That sounds like a great plan to me. What would a great week look like specifically if you "focused on demand generation?"

John (salesperson): Maybe if I dedicated two half days, from 9:00–12:00 each Thursday and Friday, that might help. We will start finding new opportunities if I save this time and complete eight half-day sessions a month for the next couple of months. I love doing demand generation on a Friday, because everyone I reach out to is in a good mood on a Friday.

Mark (sales leader): That sounds like a great plan, John. Let's do it. We can circle back and track progress at our next one-on-one.

The example above looks like a long, drawn-out way of getting to a simple demand-generation plan for John's territory. Of course, it would be much faster if Mark simply *told* John, "You're not doing enough demand generation and need to block off two half days per week to dedicate to doing it. Does that sound good, John?"

Faster, yes, but far less likely that John will do it. The assess, question, and align approach to leadership takes more time but empowers the individual. John will own the plan.

As a sales leader, you will realize that there are some one-on-one meetings you look forward to and some that you don't. Generally, you won't look forward to one-on-ones with people who are not growth oriented. These team members may become passively (or actively) aggressive in the meeting and push back on your attempts to coach and lead. These same individuals will often not prepare appropriately and have trouble articulating and committing to a set plan. Another calling card of these meetings is that they are often riddled with excuses for underperformance.

This is where your one-on-one meetings become the "canary in a coal mine," identifying wrong-fit players on the sales team. This structured sales management system will help wrong-fit teammates self-select out of the company or make it very clear that you will need to help them move on.

The Team Sales Meeting

The team sales meeting is about sharing best practices and insights among the team and elevating motivation and engagement.

In many ways, the profession of sales can be isolating. With so much of the workforce being remote today, combined with the fact that outside salespeople are constantly traveling, it is natural for salespeople to feel like they are fighting a lonely battle without anyone to support them. This is why team sales meetings are so important.

Use the team sales meeting to help your salespeople feel connected to the company and each other. Encourage team members to share success stories, best practices, and industry insights to help educate and elevate the whole team.

Here is my recommended structure for the sales team meeting:

Team Meeting Summary

Objective	• Recommit to the sales activities and objectives that will drive success. • Share news from the field (customers, prospects, industry). • Collaborate on key learnings/strategies/tactics for sales success. • Share company news and updates—leader.

Agenda	• The Numbers:
	  • Sales leader to review performance versus quota year-to-date and for the most recent period (with a positive focus) for the entire sales team.
	• Sales Team Roundtable (five minutes per salesperson)
	  • commitment for this period (both activities and results)
	  • top three priorities for this period
	  • help required
	• Collaboration/Key Learnings
	  • Identify two or three topics to discuss as a team (e.g., demand-generation strategies, market trends, or customer insights).

Desired Outcomes	• The salesperson has developed an effective game plan for the next period. • Both the sales leader and the salesperson are aligned on the plan. • The sales rep is committed to their plan.

Time in the Field Coaching Salespeople

You can't teach someone to ride a bike from a manual. Time in the field coaching is a critical aspect of elevating the performance art of professional sales. However, salespeople might be hesitant to get your coaching in the field.

At times, salespeople will avoid booking meetings in the field with you with soft excuses like, "I'm waiting for the perfect meeting!" Avoid this by booking time with your sales team even before they have the client/prospect meetings booked.

I like booking two half or full days per week "in the field." If I manage eight salespeople (and most sales leaders do), I will tell each one that I will be in the field with them for two weeks from Wednesday to "keep me busy." They can then go about the process of making sure that we have good meetings or sales calls to run together.

Big Deal Reviews

Salespeople across multiple industries tend to focus all their attention on the technical solution and pricing, and not enough time on the actual sales strategy to win the deal. **Remember:** 39 percent of the time, the buyer selects the company that sold better versus the company with the best price, quality, or service feature.

Our "big deal review" management practice is a weekly or biweekly event to collaborate as a sales team on some of our largest or most important pending deals:

Big Deal Review Meeting Summary

Purpose	<ul><li>Assess our strategic positioning on our most critical pending deals.</li><li>Collaborate with the team on options to improve our chances of winning.</li><li>Align on the next steps to apply some of the advice and feedback shared.</li></ul>
Attendees	<ul><li>Weekly or biweekly attendance is requested.</li><li>Deals are selected by the sales leader one week in advance.</li><li>Attendees can vary, but you want additional perspectives on how to win the pending deal so that attendees can include other salespeople or technical, marketing, operation, and executive team members. In addition to the salesperson who owns the deal, you want at least three and no more than six others.</li></ul> Agenda is driven by the salesperson. Leverage the ITF Deal Strategy Builder to drive the discussion. To download the ITF Deal Strategy Builder, go here: https://www.inthefunnel.com/ltls-sales-tools *Password: thesellingwell* <ul><li>ITF Deal Strategy Builder and meeting agenda should be circulated to all attendees twenty-four hours in advance of the meeting.</li></ul>

Agenda	Deal summary: ten minutes—salesperson who owns the deal: • Use the ITF Strategy Builder template. Clarification questions: ten minutes—all attendees: • Ask nonjudgmental clarification questions of the salesperson to provide additional context. Develop recommendations: five minutes—all attendees: • Write down the three things the salesperson could do to improve their strategic positioning on the deal. Share recommendations: ten minutes—all attendees/roundtable: • Ask each attendee to share their three suggestions while the salesperson running the deal captures all of the feedback on a physical or digital whiteboard that all can see. Post-meeting summary: salesperson who owns the deal: • Email all attendees, summarizing all of the recommendations received and listing the actions that they have decided to act on.
Desired Outcomes	The salesperson leading our most important deals gets ideas from "clean eyes" on potential next steps to improve their chances of winning.

It's important that everyone who joins must share feedback and the salesperson in charge captures the input. Of course, this doesn't mean the salesperson must do everything suggested, but they must at least write it down. You want to show the attendees that their feedback is valued.

Pro Tip: Ensure this meeting is a collaborative "whiteboard" session on how to change the future, not a meeting to chastise the salesperson on what they have or haven't done. If these big deal strategy sessions become a public reprimand, they will become far less effective.

Quarterly Sales Kickoffs

Every quarter, we suggest a more significant team meeting. The "quarterly sales kickoff" is another group meeting, but since there are only four per year, it offers an opportunity for a more significant reset on the sales playbook for executive leadership, sales leadership, and the sales team.

For this type of event (between one and two days), depending on the size of your company and your sales team, you will schedule more significant updates from management and the salespeople. In addition, you'll invite other executive team members (finance, product, operations, delivery, marketing, etc.) to join this kickoff to stay abreast of what the sales team is up to; it also helps them develop some empathy for how truly difficult selling for a living is.

These quarterly events are also an excellent opportunity for group sales training of the sales team (and *yes,* IN THE FUNNEL would be happy to help organize and facilitate).

Bringing sales team members from other cities and counties into town for these quarterly events and setting up some social activities for them (events, dinners, etc.) is significantly beneficial.

We also suggest using the quarterly kickoff as an opportunity to train the team.

Here is my recommended structure for the quarterly sales kickoff:

Quarterly Sales Kickoff Meeting Summary

Objective	• Share each salesperson's plan to maximize revenue from their sales territory for the coming quarter. • Collaborate on key learnings/strategies/tactics for sales success.

Agenda	• Opening Comments: Sales Leader
	  • Year-to-date summary and review
	• Sales Rep Updates: 20 to 30 minutes per rep
	  • Quarterly sales commitment with specific deals
	  • Quarterly upside potential with specific deals
	  • Quarterly activity goals re: new logo targets and current client health checks
	  • Team feedback on each sales rep's plan
	• Team training workshop (content TBD)

Desired Outcomes	• The sales team is excited and engaged for the coming period. • Successful best practices are shared among the team. • The sales team is "in the know" regarding important news about the company. • Each team member has a success plan to drive positive progress.

Here's an example email informing the sales team of the agenda. Please note that the "workshops" were training sessions that ITF facilitated on behalf of the customer.

Draft Email Note to Prepare the Team for the Quarterly Sales Kickoff

Team,

Top-tier sales performance always starts with great planning and preparation.

*In keeping with our **Call to Action** to dramatically exceed 30 percent year-over-year sales growth, we look forward to our Q3 Sales Kickoff.*

Meeting Objective

***Workshop** your detailed plans to maximize sales growth and exceed quotas in Q3.*
***Collaborate** as a team on best practices (strategies, tactics, tools).*
***Learn** sales best practices associated with:*
- *Sales Strategy*
- *Sales Call Planning*
- *Customer Health Check Meetings*

Each sales team (account executives and customer success leader) will:
- *Present their plans to the group—fifteen minutes.*
- *Leverage the room for feedback—fifteen minutes.**Please:***
- *Dry run your presentation with me three days prior.*
- *Circulate your final plans twenty-four hours in advance.*

Thanks, Mark

CHAPTER SUMMARY

- The demands on a sales leader's time are relentless because they work with the three toughest stakeholders in business: customers, salespeople, executive teams.
- Sales leaders need a disciplined sales management system to ensure they dedicate enough time, energy, and focus to the things that will have the greatest positive impact on the future behaviors of the sales team.
- The *what* of sales leadership is influencing the future performance of the sales team in a positive way.
- The *how* is the ITF sales management system.
- The ITF sales management system includes:
  - quarterly sales kickoff meetings
  - one-on-one meetings
  - team sales meetings
  - coaching time in the field
  - big deal reviews
  - win/loss reviews
- Everyone should be clear on the objective, agenda, and desired outcome from all meetings in advance.

CONCLUSION

"It's not enough to do your best; you must know what to do and then do your best."

This insightful quote by W. Edwards Deming, a pioneer of the modern quality movement, encapsulates the essence of effective action and knowing specifically what it takes to be successful.

So, where do we go from here?

First and foremost, I want to thank you for reading this book. Your reaching this conclusion is a testament to your commitment and curiosity. Many individuals who pick up nonfiction books never make it to the end. Thank you!

Mark Twain once said, "The secret to getting ahead is getting started." I sometimes struggle with overplanning and perfectionism, which can be impediments if left unchecked. Adopting the mantra of "progress, not perfection" has immensely benefited me, and I encourage you to approach your learning journey with the same mindset—just get started.

As James Clear says in *Atomic Habits*, "Changes that seem small and unimportant at first will compound into remarkable results if you're willing to stick with them for years."[30]

Yes, I suggest you continue refining your sales strategies, tactics, tools, and processes for years.

B2B sales is not just a job; it's a profession that is significant in businesses and economies.

The best professionals in various fields—law, medicine, entrepreneurship, or athletics—never stop learning. They possess a growth mindset, believing that their skills and abilities can be cultivated through effort and dedication rather than being fixed attributes.

This growth mindset isn't merely a recipe for success; it's essential for professional happiness. Carol Dweck's research in *Mindset: The New Psychology of Success* highlights how a fixed mindset can lead to higher levels of depression due to setbacks and perceived incompetence.[31]

We can learn to love selling.

Many sales leaders, professionals, and entrepreneurs don't really enjoy selling because they lack a systematic approach. They don't know what to do, and it's difficult to find joy in something you aren't good at.

Sales is not just a discipline; it's the most critical business function. Mastering sales can future-proof careers, amplify business value, and empower professionals to achieve new heights.

To "sell well," you need more than enthusiasm; you need a strategic playbook. This book offers precisely that—a researched, insightful system to enhance your sales capabilities and drive better outcomes for your clients.

By applying this sales playbook to your territory now, you'll witness an improvement in your sales results and a renewed passion for your work. A structured approach to sales grants you greater control over your professional journey, paving the way toward mastery.

Thank you once again for embarking on this journey of growth and learning. Remember, this book is just the beginning. Continuously develop your mindset, skill set, and tool set in professional sales, and embrace the joy of selling—it's not just a career; it's a path to fulfillment and success.

NEXT STEPS

- Please go and download all of the free tools that we have provided as a bonus for buying this book.
    - They can be found here: https://www.inthefunnel.com/ltls-sales-tools (please use the password "thesellingwell")
- Connect with me on LinkedIn and follow our latest insights and best practices to help.
    - https://www.linkedin.com/in/markandrewcox/
- Join us for an in-person or virtual remote professional sales workshop, whether you're a sales leader, salesperson, or sales development rep.
    - https://www.inthefunnel.com/sales-workshops
- Reach out to me personally with any questions about the content of this book.
    - markcox@inthefunnel.com

GLOSSARY

Account Management: The process of nurturing and maintaining relationships with existing clients.

Approach Call: An initial conversation between a salesperson and a prospect to create attention, awareness, and interest in your product or service. This call aims to learn about the prospect's desired business outcomes and share your company's value proposition.

B2B (Business-to-Business): Sales transactions that occur between businesses rather than between a business and a consumer.

B2C (Business-to-Consumer): Sales transactions that occur between a business and an individual consumer.

Benefits: The advantages or positive outcomes that a product or service provides to the customer.

Buyer's Journey: The process that customers go through when making a purchasing decision, including exploring, evaluating, engaging, and experiencing. It is attributed to Frank Cespedes.

Buyer/Buying Persona: A semi-fictional representation of an ideal customer based on market research and data.

Call Blitz: A concentrated effort by a sales team to make a large number of sales calls within a short period.

Call-to-Action (CTA): A prompt that encourages the reader or viewer to take a specific action, such as making a purchase or contacting a sales representative.

Churn Rate: The rate at which salespeople transition out of a company or the rate at which customers churn out from your business.

Closing: The final stage of the sales process where a deal is successfully completed, and the customer commits to purchasing.

Closing Ratio: The percentage of sales opportunities that result in closed deals.

Cold Calling: Making unsolicited calls to potential customers with whom the salesperson has had no prior contact. Also known as demand generation or prospecting.

Commission: A percentage of sales revenue or a fixed amount paid to salespeople as compensation for achieving sales performance targets.

Competitive Analysis: Evaluation of competitors' strengths and weaknesses to identify opportunities for differentiation.

Consultative Selling: An approach to sales that focuses on understanding the customer's needs and exploring potential solutions.

Conversion Rate: The percentage of leads or prospects that move to each progressive stage of the sales process.

CRM (Customer Relationship Management): Software or systems used to manage interactions with current and potential customers.

Cross-Selling: The practice of selling additional products or services to existing customers.

Decision Criteria: The factors or considerations that influence a customer's decision-making process.

Decision-Maker: The person within an organization who has the authority to make purchasing decisions.

Demographics: Statistical data relating to the population and particular groups within it, such as age, gender, income, etc.

Elevator Pitch: A concise and persuasive summary of a product, service, or business idea that can be delivered in the time it takes to ride an elevator.

Features: The specific characteristics or attributes of a product or service.

Forecasting: The process of predicting future sales based on the status of sales opportunities.

Gatekeeper: A person, typically a receptionist or assistant, who controls access to decision-makers within an organization.

Follow-Up: Continued communication with a prospect or customer after an initial interaction.

Inbound Marketing: A strategy that focuses on attracting customers through content creation, social media, and search engine optimization.

Key Performance Indicators (KPIs): Quantifiable metrics used to evaluate the success of a sales team or individual.

Lead Generation: The process of identifying and attracting potential customers.

Lead Nurturing: The process of building relationships with potential customers at every stage of the sales funnel.

Objection Handling: Techniques used to address and overcome customer concerns or resistance during the sales process.

Needs Analysis: A thorough assessment of a prospect's requirements, challenges, and goals to determine the best solution.

Pareto Principle: 80/20 rule: The principle that roughly 80 percent of results come from 20 percent of causes or efforts.

Pipeline: The visual representation of all sales opportunities and their respective stages in the sales process. Also known as funnel. Hence the name of our company, IN THE FUNNEL. Thank you, Donna Radia-Cox!

Pipeline Management: The process of tracking and managing sales opportunities throughout the sales cycle.

Pitch: A persuasive presentation of a product or service's features, benefits, and value proposition. Don't pitch at customers...PLEASE.

Prospect: A potential customer who has expressed interest in a product or service but has not yet made a purchase.

Qualification: The process of determining whether a lead or prospect meets the criteria for being a viable sales opportunity and meetings the criteria of your Ideal Customer Profile.

Qualified Lead: A prospect who meets the criteria for being a viable sales opportunity and meets the criteria for your Ideal Customer Profile.

Referral: A recommendation or introduction provided by a satisfied customer or business contact.

Retention: The ability to keep existing customers satisfied and loyal to the company.

Sales Funnel: The visual representation of the sales process, from creating demand to closing the sale.

Sales Quota: A predetermined sales target that a salesperson is expected to achieve within a specific time frame.

Sales Territory: A geographical area assigned to a salesperson or sales team for prospecting and selling activities.

Solution Selling: A sales approach that focuses on understanding the customer's problems and offering tailored solutions.

Target Audience: The specific group of people or businesses that a product or service is intended to reach.

Upselling: The practice of persuading customers to purchase a more expensive, expansive, or upgraded version of a product or service.

Value Proposition: A statement that communicates what you do as a business, the desired business outcomes that you provide customers, and your competitive differentiation in your markets.

Warm Lead: A prospect who has shown interest or expressed a need for a product or service.

ABOUT THE AUTHOR

Mark Cox has sold, structured, and negotiated some of the largest single-sale transactions in North America, including a billion-dollar transaction with a top-ten US bank.

After twenty-plus years working for large corporations leading sales teams, Mark founded IN THE FUNNEL (ITF) Sales Coaching with the mission to dramatically improve the performance of business-to-business sales teams and, in doing so, improve the lives of professional salespeople.

With a focus on strategy, process, tools, mindset, and discipline, Mark has helped hundreds of companies achieve predictable, double-digit sales growth by implementing ITF's proprietary Sales Playbook.

Mark was named one of the leading sales consultants of 2021 by *Selling Power* magazine. He is also a partner with the Canadian Professional Sales Association, and all ITF training content is officially accredited by CPSA. Mark hosts the top-rated *The Selling Well podcast* where he interviews some of the top minds in the world on professional selling, leadership, coaching, and mindset.

When not coaching customers to sell better, Mark can be found goal-tending in local hockey rinks, fitness training, or playing drums in his nineties-rock cover band.

markcox@inthefunnel.com
linkedin.com/in/markandrewcox/
inthefunnel.com

REFERENCES

1   US Bureau of Labor Statistics, "Occupational Employment and Wages,"
    news release, May 2023, https://www.bls.gov/news.release/ocwage.t01.
    htm. See Table 1, which is available at https://www.bls.gov/news.release/
    ocwage.t01.htm. The OES data shows 13.3 million people in "Sales and
    related occupations and another 575,000 'Sales Managers.'" However, this
    survey excludes the approximately 15 million self-employed people in
    the United States, perhaps 20 percent of which could be considered in
    professional sales.

2   Frank V. Cespedes, *Sales Management That Works: How to Sell in a World That
    Never Stops Changing* (Boston: Harvard Business Review Press, 2021).

3   Suzanne Fogel et al., "Teaching Sales," *Harvard Business Review* (July/August
    2012), https://hbr.org/2012/07/teaching-sales.

4   RepVue, "RepVue Cloud Sales Index: Q3 2023," https://www.repvue.com/
    cloud-index/2023/Q3.

5   Gartner, "Sales Motivation: How to Empower
    and Retain Your Sellers," accessed June 24,
    2024, https://www.gartner.com/en/sales/topics/sales-motivation.

6   The Bridge Group, *CRO Characteristics & Comp Research (Hudson, MA: The
    Bridge Group, 2024).*

7   Brent Adamson and Nick Toman, "5 Ways the Future of B2B Buying
    Will Rewrite the Rules of Effective Selling," *Gartner Research, August 4,
    2020,* https://www.gartner.com/en/documents/3988440.

8   Hermann Ebbinghaus, *Uber das Gedachtnis* (Berlin: University of Berlin Press, 1885).

9   Matthew Dixon and Ted McKenna, *The Jolt Effect: How High Performers Overcome Customer Indecision* (New York: Portfolio/Penguin, 2022).

10 Jaynie Smith, *Relevant Selling* (Fort Lauderdale: Executive Suite Press, Inc., 2012).

11 Robert Cialdini, *Influence: The Psychology of Persuasion* (New York: HarperCollins, 1984).

12 Aaron Ross and Marylou Tyler, *Predictable Revenue: Turn Your Business into a Sales Machine with the $100 Million Best Practices of Salesforce.com* (Pebblestorm, 2011).

13 Nick Morgan, *Can You Hear Me? How to Connect with People in a Virtual World* (Boston: Harvard Business Review Press, 2018.

14 Cialdini, Influence.

15 Justin Michael, *Sales Superpowers: A New Outbound Operating System to Drive Explosive Pipeline Growth* (Phoenix: Jones Media Publishing, 2024).

16 Diana I. Tamir and Jason P. Mitchell, "Disclosing Information about the Self Is Intrinsically Rewarding," PNAS 109, no. 21 (May 22, 2012): 8038–43, https://www.pnas.org/doi/full/10.1073/pnas.1202129109.

17 Diane Hamilton, Cracking the Curiosity Code: The Key to Unlocking Human Potential (Dr. Diane Hamilton, LLC, 2018).

18 Andy Paul, Sell without Selling Out: A Guide to Success on Your Own Terms (Page Two, 2022).

19 Cespedes, *Sales Management That Works.*

20 Jeff Davis, "How Sales Can Win before 57% of the Buyers Journey Is Over," LinkedIn Sales Blog, March 27, 2018, https://www.linkedin.com/business/

sales/blog/b2b-sales/how-sales-can-win-before-57--of-the-buyers-journey-is-over. This CEB stat shows how far through the buyer's journey they are before engaging salespeople.

21   Dianne Ledingham, Mark Kovac, Heidi Locke Simon, "The New Science of Sales Force Productivity," *Harvard Business Review* (September 2006), https://hbr.org/2006/09/the-new-science-of-sales-force-productivity?autocomplete=true.

22   Justin Michael and Tony Hughes, Tech-Powered Sales: Achieve Superhuman Sales Skills (Nashville: HarperCollins Leadership, 2021).

23   Cespedes, Sales Management That Works.

24   Geoff Smart and Randy Street, *WHO: The A Method for Hiring* (New York: Random House, 2008).

25   Daniel Pink, *When: The Scientific Secrets of Perfect Timing* (New York: Riverhead Books, 2018).

26   Manny Medina, Max Altschuler, and Mark Kosoglow, Sales Engagement: How the World's Fastest-Growing Companies Are Modernizing Sales through Humanization at Scale (Hoboken, NJ: John Wiley & Sons, 2019).

27   Daniel Goleman, "Leadership That Gets Results," *Harvard Business Review* (March/April 2000), https://hbr.org/2000/03/leadership-that-gets-results.

28   Liz Wiseman, Multipliers: How the Best Leaders Make Everyone Smarter (New York: Harper Business, 2010).

29   Fogel et al., "Teaching Sales."

30   James Clear, Atomic Habits: An Easy & Proven Way to Build Good Habits & Break Bad Ones (New York: Avery, 2018).

31   Carol Dweck, Mindset: The New Psychology of Success (New York: Ballantine Books, 2006).

Made in the USA
Columbia, SC
16 August 2024

40542900R00122